In the Company of Strangers ...

Also by Richard Trembath

More Lives Than One (Pre-Press Concepts, 1996)

In the Company of Strangers ...

Richard Trembath

First published by Busybird Publishing 2015

Copyright © 2015 Richard Trembath

ISBN 978-1-925260-95-3

This book is copyright. Apart from any fair dealing for the purposes of study, research, criticism, review, or as otherwise permitted under the Copyright Act, no part may be reproduced by any process without written permission. Enquiries should be made through the publisher.

Typesetting: Busybird Publishing
www.busybird.com.au

Author photo by Kathleen Trembath

Acknowledgments

There are many people whose presence in my life, whose faith in me, and whose help have enabled this book to become a reality. Without their individual and collective support, encouragement, patience and inspiration, the works which make up these pages would have remained with the other assorted souvenirs of my life 'in the bottom drawer'.

They know who they are but among them special thanks is due to the late Sam Bickford, who started it all; to Peter Byrne and the late Nancy Helmore, who gave it the impetus it needed; to Deverie De Ron and my daughter, Fiona Trembath, for their unfailing support and wise counsel; to the late Keith McGowan and Mavis Ellis for their professionalism, talent and passion; to Jennette O'Mahoney for her inspiration; to my son Jeffrey Trembath and the late Christine Mogford for the part they played in making it happen and to my publisher, Blaise van Hecke, for her patience and guidance in the transition from manuscript to final product.

Contents

Poems

The Life We Live
In The Company Of Strangers	3
Party Decoration	4
Our Winter Lives	6
But Once	8
Not While We Care	12
Life's Path	13
Too Short	14

Along The Journey
In The Shadow Of Ben Bulben	16
Sunset On The Zambesi	17
The Tree On Gibbet Hill	18

Facing The Years
Desolation	22
When Dark November's O'er	23
Introspection	24
While Love Remains	26
Within the Soft Night's Warm Embrace	28

Moments
When We Were Twenty-One	30
In The Velvet Night	31
When Did the Roses Die?	34
The Day We Walked Away	36
We Have Grown Old	37
It Wasn't There Before	38
Without You	40

Candles	43
The Graceless Night	44
A Bunch Of Yellow Roses	46
The Seasons Of Our Love	47

Reflections
Where We Live	50
Addictions	51
Corporate Irrelevance	52
The Journey	53

Stories

Truth	55
A Mug's Game	59
The Feast Of Stephen	81
The Race	91
Four-Letter 'L' Words	97
A Breeder's Lament	119
Catherine In Wonderland	125
From Insult To Injury	131
Only Mugs Try At Trials	135
Rest Easy, Girl	139
Copyright Acknowledgments	147

The Life We Live
Poems

In The Company Of Strangers

*We live our lives in the company
of strangers:*

How little we know of the hearts
of the men who surround us;
How seldom we see but a glimpse
of another man's soul.
We each tread our own destined journey
that only we know of,
And strangers pass strangers, all bound
for the bell's final toll.

'Tis seldom we know of another man's
thoughts or his essence,
Only he can decide what he shows us
and wants us to see,
And if he decides to guard secrets and
keep his own counsel,
He will never be known to the world,
nor to you, nor to me.

We're alone when we start on life's
journey wherever it takes us,
And alone we will be, yet again,
when we come to its end,
And in transit our lives are surrounded
on all sides by strangers,
And the best we can hope for
is one we can truly call friend.

Party Decoration

When do we cut the ribbons which connect us,
cease the pretence
of wishing to be the pillars of society,
respected,
looked upon as 'proper' by our peers
– 'the way we should be'?

When do we let go,
release our grip
on what we're taught are principles,
and they their grip on us?

Is it too late for our return
to basic instincts,
those which lie in wait
but shrouded
by 'the done and proper thing' –

Man's pomp and babble –
cluttered now by overgrowth,
a tightly woven net
from which escape
becomes progressively less possible?

What holds us from our instincts –
lust, survival, will to live?
from blood and water,
warmth
and basic love?

When will we cease to care
what other people think
and live our lives not by indoctrination,
but rather
by what instinct taught us
as we left the womb?

And when will we discard
the 'window dressing',
that which makes us what we are
(or have become)
and robs us yet of what we truly are.

Courage, my friends,
and focus!
The world is so enamoured
of the illusion it creates
it can no longer recognise the truth
behind society's façade.
Ashes, dust,
flesh, blood and lust
— these alone are real.

The rest is fluff.
Inherited tradition.

Party decoration.

Our Winter Lives

They disappear more quickly in the
colder, barren climes
Where snow falls steadily and
covers them:
Two sets of footprints, yours and mine.

The snow blends, flake by drifting flake,
to cover them
And forms a pristine blanket, uncaring
where it falls and totally
Without discrimination.

Yesterday's snow, and all the indentations
which we made, together
In our lives, are gone,
with ne'er a trace that they were ever there.

The winding path – the one we trod –
is but a memory;
A fleeting recollection of a happy time,
but gone, to whence such memories go.

And now, that is its all – a memory –
and no-one cares whose memory, or why,
For that was yesterday.

But now it is another day, which brings
a new, fresh, pristine path, which all
Of us can choose to take; our chance to make
new footprints in the snow.

The choice is ours to write the text
of our new lives on Nature's
Clean white overlay, or, if we will,
withdraw, to dwell instead upon the loss
Of footprints made on other days; made
yesterday – and gone.

It matters not:

Too soon the sun – God's fiery orb –
will deem 'Enough!' It will be over.
And all the little secrets of our winter lives
will join the raging torrent as
It rushes headlong down the gorge
to join the summer sea.

But Once

Softness, grace, and beauty,
Peace,
Where have they gone?

Where are the days of yesterday,
The happy carefree days
Of laughter,
Hopes and joy,
The brief tranquillity
Once almost captured
Yet let slip, and lost
And ne'er revisited?

Yes, what is gone is truly gone
And yesterday is over
And its joy, if there was joy,
Is just a memory.
We know within us
Oft' we say we shall return,
'Next time', we say,
But next time never comes.

We get one chance alone
And each one lost is gone
And, ne'er can be regained,
But each one held, and
Savored, be it oh so brief,
Is beauty, truth, unblemished gold,
A crystal moment of magnificence,
Perfection,
And an insight
Brief, provided into what
Makes this life so.

We must live now, while love is here
And full and bursting forth to bloom,
For all too soon today
Is yesterday
And love, and life,
The chance to live,
Has passed us by.

So grasp, and hold
And live life now,
Not 'next time'
For those words belong
To cowards, they
Who let
Life's river flow on by
And ne'er become a part of it
And hide from life, to get it
Over with.

But truth is here, somewhere
Amidst the mire,
Peace, tranquillity,
Beyond the throng,
The noise, the cold
Hard world that hems us in,
Oppresses us where'er we look.
Beauty comes;
Not often,
But it comes.

But we too oft' ignore it
And make not
The most of these, our opportunities,
Our share of life's true nature
We avoid, side-step them
Or, worse still, we fail
To recognise them, so intent
Are we
On following the narrow paths
Of daily life.

To each shall come
The vision, clarity of sight
To recognise, if only once,
The beauty, and the soaring heights
Of joy that this world holds,
But, when passed by, each moment wasted
Goes,
And having gone
Is lost beyond recall, unlived,
And shall not come again.

And some lives pass
Unlived
From dust, through flesh and life,
To dust,

Unknowing what life holds
Beyond their clouded field
Of vision,
Never knowing beauty, truth or peace
And never knowing love.

He is no man, the man
Who passes by this way
With head held low, and
Mind
Ne'er asking: 'What is this life all about?'
He breathes, he walks, he talks
Yet leaves no mark of having
Passed,
Or having lived at all.

I shall not go this way, for I
Shall have but this
One life,
And I shall, from this day,
Seek all these things that go
To make the essence
Of this life
And I shall live
Each moment for itself,
And life
Shall not elude me.

Not While We Care

These days will one day be
'the good old days',
– but ah! not yet.

Not while we have the fire,
the strength of sinew,
surge of blood ...
Not while our minds still seek,
inquire,
and pursue.
Not while we care
and have the strength of will
to make that caring matter.

We will look back, one day,
upon these days,
but from the distance:
from beyond Life's battlefield,
upon the high-ground,
whence life's plain can be surveyed.
With some regrets ...? perhaps,
but they o'erwhelmed
with pride;
with satisfaction at a fight
well fought
and at a battle won.

Life's Path

You pluck'd me from woe's icy grip
And warmed my life again,
My soul repaired, my strength renew'd,
You dull'd my mortal pain,
You made the storm clouds roll away,
You made the sky seem blue,
You calmed my shuddering, aching heart
And built my faith anew.

But life's paths do not always lead
Where we would like them to;
The path we plan and that we walk
We often find are two.
But moments cherished, moments shared,
Will last beyond the day
And though fate's twists encumber them
They will not fade away.

'Tis difficult sometimes to grasp
That all we have is now,
But well I know naught barr'd the way
Unto life's brink but thou.
These days we will remember, Love,
Not for their parting's pain,
But love, and truth, the joy we shared,
Which shall be ours again.

Too Short

How sad it is to die
knowing you
completed everything:
All you ever set out
to complete,
in life
and in the world.

To know you had
sufficient time,
too much,
and that you utilised it
– never took a moment
to indulge yourself
or just be lazy.
Never felt frustrated
at a task
unfinished.

Never realised
our time here is
too short:
Too short to stick
the photos in the album.
Too short to write
the story of our lives.
Too short to
'tidy up the ends'
and realise all
our cherished dreams.

Along the Journey
Poems

for Frank Hearns

In The Shadow Of Ben Bulben

To vivid County Sligo, by great Ben Bulben's side
That final day of summer, from distant Malahide
To the church of St. Columba, where history abounds,
Where the poet Yeats lies sleeping in the cold and stony ground,
I made my pilgrim's journey, through Ireland's verdant land,
To where the great Armada first touched the windswept sand;
I saw the age-old splendour of the beautiful Lough Key,
Of Lough Arrow and Lough Gill and the Isle of Innesfree,
By the picture-perfect country lanes that wind by Lake Glencar,
The majestic hidden waterfall, the valley from afar;
I passed the Gaelic Chieftain, alone atop the hill
And ancient Boyle Abbey, crumbling, yet defiant still:
I stood in Drumcliff's churchyard with its memories of Yeats
And doubted not that peace he found beyond his heaven's gates,
For fortunate a life he lived 'neath Ireland's misty sky
In the shadow of Ben Bulben 'til his horseman passed on by.

Sunset On The Zambesi

At sunset the elephants come
in the distant haze,
silhouetted in the gathering dusk,
down to the water's edge, to drink.

The sun, an incandescent globe
of burnished orange,
defiant in its last moments,
sinks, first slowly, behind the palm trees,
lingers ...
then suddenly is gone,
leaving each one stark
against the sky,
its tip fringed
with God's golden flame.

The land engulfs the glorious orb
but leaves its brilliant, fragile legacy.

As we glide, silently,
upon the broad, majestic river,
we watch the intrinsic hues
fade slowly ... imperceptibly ...
until at last we gaze no more
and know the day has finally
succumbed
unto the velvet cloak of night.

On a hill beside the main Hobart road, 20km south of Launceston, stands a lone tree. It was on this tree that, during the days when Tasmania was a penal colony in the early 1800s, the bodies of executed criminals were hung as a deterrent to passers-by.

The Tree On Gibbet Hill

BENEATH your dying, splintered boughs
'Midst rocks the horses graze,
Your broken, withered limbs give not
A hint of earlier days,
Days when you bore your dreadful fruit,
When human life you craved,
When haunted, hell-bound sinners you
Denied the very grave.

The days when you defiant stood,
A warning to the land,
Of Mankind's inhumanity
And Death's swift icy hand;
The ghost of one such tortured soul
They say lurks with you still
And curses those who scorn the dead
Who hung on Gibbet Hill.

But time is pass'd, men's ways are changed
And your dread days are o'er,
You stand, a broken monument
To times that are no more;
Perhaps when your time comes and you
Return unto the earth,
Your passing will release the souls
And grant them second birth.

The highwayman, the murderer,
The fool, the thief, the cheat,
Who rotted on your boughs denied
The sinner's crimson sheet,
Denied in death the dignity
Of but a pauper's hole,
Perhaps your death at last will grant
Repose unto his soul.

And you will be a legend, voiceless,
Lingering in the night,
With no man left to tell your tale
And naught to mark your site.
The land shall know tranquillity,
The lost soul's voice be still,
As horses yet unborn graze 'midst
The rocks on Gibbet Hill.

Facing The Years
Poems

Desolation

Emptiness.

How deep the well that plummets
into nothingness.

How bitter the soft tears I cry
alone.

How black the night that brings not
comfort, nor repose.

How hideous the blinding light of dawn
that brings another day
whose only purpose is
to torture me.

How heavy this cold stone
that is my heart.

I know not how to face today,
much less the years to come.

When Dark November's O'er

No flower blooms upon your grave
Though roses grow each side,
I love you both, who gave me life,
My tears I cannot hide.

Together now in death you sleep
As once in life you lay,
My memory still is clear and true
On this memorial day.

Your short lives ended all too soon
For me to know you well;
Yet in their springtime when they heard
The tolling of death's bell.

How can I know if your pure love
Stays with you evermore?
Perhaps your rose will bloom again
When dark November's o'er.

Written on the occasion of a visit by the author to the grave of his parents on November 23, 1996, the 44th anniversary of the death of his father.

Introspection

It can be a great discomfort,
being loved:
To know another's being
revolves around your own.
To feel responsible,
to feel obliged,
and be unsure of whether
what you feel for them
is really love
or just a warm and pleasant
sense of obligation.

It's said that when love comes,
you'll know,
and doubtless that is true.
But what of those whose
soul of love lies wounded
and beyond repair?
Surrounded by stone walls, built
by that inner instinct which,
try as it might,
seeks naught but
mere survival?

Can love alone revive
the soul
that hesitates to love?
Who knows? – not I:
Sometimes I wonder if,
perhaps, 'tis better
to be loved than be
the one in love;
if maybe it is better to receive
love unconditional
than be in love.

While Love Remains

We are never apart as long
as I have memories of you
And you of me:

We are never apart as long
as we can recall
The things we shared.

For as long as our memories
endure and we care,
The bond will remain.

We shall never be apart for
as long as memories shared
Are cherished by us both.

Though land and water
may separate us,
They cannot separate our hearts,

For the Earth extends from
where I am to where you are
And it is the same Earth:

I can touch it where I am and
you where you are
And the Earth will link our touch.

I can look at the moon and
know that you are looking
At the same moon:

I can drift through time and
know it is the same time
I drift through with you.

We shall never be apart for
as long as love remains:
We shall never be alone.

Within The Soft Night's Warm Embrace

Hid by woman's precious arc
there lurks the dreaded spectre dark
and waits to strike where ego lies,
the arc for which the newborn cries.

'Tis not her being, nor her soul
and yet it is what makes her whole,
which fears the swift and healing blade
that elsewhere sees her unafraid.

She rises up, hark! hear her voice:
'Be strong, ye faithful, and rejoice!
The choice is ours and we, as one,
choose life and do what must be done.

Repel the Reaper! Strike the foe!
Cry loud: 'Tis not my turn to go!'
Then reassume thy former grace
within the soft night's warm embrace.

Moments
Poems

When We Were Twenty-One

I lusted after you when
we were twenty-one
But you had eyes for
another
and you went away.

My heart followed you
along the many pathways
of your life
And then one day, finally,
you noticed me.

But even as you did,
both of us knew
that we could not go back
in time
And that our golden chance
had passed us by.

In The Velvet Night

The sky is clear tonight, the moon is full
And all the stars twinkle bright
Against the backdrop of
The velvet night
And I am here with you, content
To be alone together and to share
The glory of the night, the stars,
The murmur of the breeze, the peace,
Tranquillity
Of this night shared.
This night, so brief,
An instant in our lives
But so important because of its
Perfection
And the fact that we are here
Together, without which
Perfection could not be.

The stars were there before us and will be
Long after we are gone,
And they shall shine on other lovers
Yet to be.
But they shall shine on none enraptured
More than we
And there shall be no night
More perfect than this night,
No love to rival what we share
And no stars shining brighter
Than our love.

The night is wondrous,
And the stars,
But we are too inclined to take them all
For granted — our inherent right,
And only lovers ever
Stop to think
Of what they are and what they mean
And why we see them now
Beneath the black and velvet sky.

And why are we together, I with you
And you with me?
What right have we to be so much
More happy than the rest
Of all mankind?

What miracle did first decree
That we should both be born
In this same era,
This same land —
That our lone paths
Should cross, and then converge —
That we should be as one
Not just in body
But in mind and spirit, one?

No longer two alone, but one
In attitude and thought
And aim
And one in all we do.
How can it be that we should be
As perfect as the night,

And yet we are, and know we are
And know that glorious though the night
May be
It pales and dulls beside
The lustre of our love.

'Tis hard to realise that when
We disappear back whence we came
Our love shall not remain
To outshine stars on other nights,
That all we really have is here
And now,
That we must grasp it, savour it,
For though it last our lifetimes
It is as a new pick'd rose
Whose beauty lingers
But a moment, then is gone.

And other loves shall come
Beneath these stars, this
Clear and cloudless sky and
This same moon
Long after we are gone,
But they shall not surpass
What we have here
Nor near approach the wonder
Of this night,
And we can wish them
Nothing greater than
That they should know
A moment of the tranquil night,
That they should be in love
As much as we
And share what we have shared.

When Did The Roses Die?

Where did they go, the golden sands,
The beach I walked with you?
Where went the sun that shone
To grace the days when our love was new?
When came the tide, whence came the clouds,
The dark, the driving rain,
The cold that now engulfs the life
That I must live in vain?

When did the roses lose their blush,
The landscape lose its hue?
When did the sun that bathed our lives
Slip silently from view?
Where went the impish, joyful light
That twinkled in your eye?
Where went the love once brave and true?
When did the roses die?

Under the scythe of the Reaper Grim
And his vile whore, Neglect,
Who noiseless come in the night and cut
A swath when we least expect,
Who make us pay for each tiny sin
And each chance that we let pass by,
And leave us, amid the shreds of our lives,
To ask: 'When did the roses die?'

Where is the joy of the days long gone
And the times I spent with you;
Of snow on the mountain and nights of rain
And strolls in the morning dew?
How did I lose you, where did you go,
When did life pass me by?
My memory still is of blood-red blooms,
When did the roses die?

The Day We Walked Away

Where have you gone?
Each way I turn the path is blocked with barricades.
Where must I look, what must I do
to find your laughter once again?
Are we so changed that 'we'
– the 'we' that once we were –
is just a half-forgotten dream?
Are we but memories of happier times,
shared joys, ambitions, plans?
How did we slide from such a peak?
When did the fledgling drift of snow
become an avalanche?
How do we turn back time and heal the wounds?
Too late? Perhaps.
But we will not forget the view that once we shared
from this life's highest peaks,
the mountain air,
the laughter in life's Spring.
You will remain a part of me and I of you
regardless of what Autumn brings
or where its narrowing paths may lead.
'Which path?' I ask – there are so many
and I know that you are there, just out of sight,
beyond the bend of one of them.
Which path? Which barricade?
In which direction did you go
the day we turned our backs and walked away?

We Have Grown Old

We have, both of us, grown old
And our beauty now
is reflected
from within
Rather than simply being there,
Resplendent.

It Wasn't There Before

How could I know what our lives held
That first day when I met you,
Yet I did.
Perhaps not straight away,
But still, not long.

Slowly realisation dawned,
Crept up on me – off-guard and unaware –
As the first light of morning creeps,
Gradually ... so imperceptibly.

The light comes,
Thin at first
But then in stronger hues
Until at last the dawn
Is there,
The dark void gone,
And no-one who has seen it knows
When it began
Or just when night succumbed to day.

It wasn't there before,
This patch of warm inside,
This joy that bubbles up
Engulfing me
When someone speaks your name,
Yet it's here now.

And I know not
Just when it was that you became
Important in my life,
But yet I know that it was not
Today, or yesterday —
It seems it's been
A thousand years.

Without You

Without you this room is just a room,
These walls are only walls.
Without you this day is just another day
And I care not about it
And notice not if it be fine, or clear or dull,
Or if it really be a day at all.
Without you I remain in limbo,
Thinking not, nor doing, and without
Ambition
Save to see your face.

Without you I am just a shell, dormant
And awaiting to be brought to life
By your mere presence,
To be enraptured by your smile
Your touch, your spoken word.
To feel the surge of life within my veins
Brought there by your existence and
The knowledge unbelievable
That you are really mine
And that you care.

These walls become a haven
And this room
The world,
And I have no desire but to be
Alone with you; alone,
Or in a crowd,
For just to be with you,
Together, is alone.
To love you and to feel the bond
Of warmth, intangible

But there,
Invisible, and yet as real
As we ourselves.
A bond of warmth and peace and confidence,
Serenity,
Which though unseen
Could not be hid from any
Who observed us.

And I care not who knows,
I want the world to know
And be a brighter, warmer place
For having known our happiness.
And if it bring some joy to those
Who walk this world without love,
Mere observers,
That can but add more lustre
To the joy
Of knowing that we have
What they have not and being
Thankful
That it came to me and you.

Why we should be the chosen
Ones I do not know:
All that I know is that we are
And that we have each other
And that all else matters not.
Before you came the world was here
And I was here
And I was, in my way, content,
Oblivious.

But now it seems unreal
To think that in those days
Before you I imagined that I knew
Of life.
My life began with you.
My life revolves around you
And exists because of you.

Without you this room is just a room,
These walls are only walls;
This world is emptiness.
Without you.

For Deverie

Candles

The silent glow flickers on your face
and is mirrored in your eyes.

Contentment, soft-edged, settles
and surrounds you
in your haven from the world.
The candles, like our lives,
burn imperceptibly
and, one by one,
they flicker, and are gone.

But they are not gone yet:
They linger still, their light endures.
Their time has not yet come.
Not yet … Not yet.

For Christine

The Graceless Night

Why are you *there* when I am here?
If you were here with me, I think I could relax and sleep:
Or maybe not.

I have gone beyond tired – I am just tired of being tired.
It makes no sense. I need to be awake when morning comes,
Not now.

Where will I find my essence and vitality
when they are needed
if they have melted, drop by drop,
and oozed into obscurity
throughout the graceless and impervious night?

Why can I not restore some form of order
to those things which know their places
and their functions
but merely wish to flout my will?

Why suddenly does no-one know the ordered rules,
nor even Lethe seek to claim her own?

The night can seize control and guide the guideless through its
dark and unforgiving byways, but be aware that those
who yet survive when comes the morn
will recognise their destinations by the light of day.

Why are you not here now so when some semblance of order
is restored, you are in readiness, prepared,
to step into the breech again, take up the reins
of leadership and steer us forth into the day?

Sleep holds us still at bay and, doing so, defeats us.
We must rest and seek our strength from those who seek
in perpetuity to yet deprive us of it.

If you were here, then sleep would come and gradually
the aged order would reform once more
and, in the heavens, craggy planets would line up,
and sleep and peace enshroud the world.

For Yada

A Bunch Of Yellow Roses

A bunch of yellow roses
Lay at my door today,
With them they brought a wish from one
Who loves from far away.

They'll bloom brief days in splendour,
Then wilt and fade and die,
But leave behind a memory
That I will ne'er deny.

A dozen yellow roses,
A token rich and rare,
Declaring with their beauty:
'I love you and I care.'

They bring with them the scent of love,
Of loyalty and pride,
Reassurance, unrequired,
Of love that will abide.

Our lives are strewn with moments
That we cherish through the years,
And roses often tell of love
And sometimes tell of tears.

But there will be no gift to touch
My heart along life's way
Like the bunch of yellow roses
That lay at my door today.

For Christine

The Seasons Of Our Love

We missed each other's Springtime
because we were elsewhere.

Then Summer came,
and left again and still you were not there.

Soft Autumn, with its mellow tones
became our own lives' Spring,

We savoured it, and dreamed our dreams
of what each day would bring.

There seemed so many happy days
ahead for us to share,

We gave no thought to Winter
— but on a sudden it was there ...

And all too soon we realized
the life we loved was gone,

The mists rolled in,
the dark clouds brought
the cold and driving rain.

You left —

I can but shelter ...
and hope we meet again.

Reflections
Poems

Where We Live

There are two time states,
the past and the future,
which fit together perfectly.

Between them, in a place
which does not exist,
is the present.

This is where we live.

Addictions

I cannot trust myself
to not do
the things
I do not want
myself
to do.

Corporate Irrelevance

We start our working lives believing
we shall be rewarded
by a grateful master:
But we learn that we are merely
cannon-fodder – pay numbers
in a computer run by people
we do not know, who are themselves
mere pay numbers in the same
computer.
Our master is but a name
– we know him not, he knows not us
and when we go
he knows not even we were there,
much less that we are gone.

The Journey

Do you ever feel as if
you've been inhaled
into the arsehole of the world?
Dark, isn't it?
No matter: try not to worry —
You'll be spat out
eventually.

Truth Stories

Truth

It is reasonable to believe that truth is absolute, like trust and virginity; either it exists or it doesn't, that something is true, absolutely, or it isn't.

But it can also be argued that there are several types of truth, none of which suffers from having qualifications attached to it.

First there is the truth which is true. There are true things which are true because they actually happened. Happening-truth.

Then there is the truth which seems to be true. There are things which seemed to happen and become true because all concerned believe absolutely that they are true.

And there is the truth which has not yet become true but which ultimately will be true. This is a truth, or a story of a truth, made up of parts, all of which are true. Story-truth. It may never have existed in a whole form, as a truth or an event which has been experienced by one person, but it is true in that its parts are true and it will, in the fullness of infinite time, exist one day as a whole, rather than as the sum of its individual parts.

Then there is what is popularly known as 'creative non-fiction'.

The 'non-fiction' part, of course, means it is true, but 'creative' means that the truth, whether a single instance or a collection of such instances, has been enhanced for the sake of making its story more cohesive and easier to tell.

This differs only marginally from story-truth in that it is a true story, creatively enhanced, rather than a collection of true parts, which have not yet happened simultaneously, but which ultimately will do so.

These stories, therefore, come in four sections:

        TRUE STORIES WHICH ARE ALREADY TRUE

        TRUE STORIES WHICH APPEAR TO BE TRUE

        TRUE STORIES WHICH ULTIMATELY WILL BE TRUE

        TRUE STORIES COUCHED IN CREATIVITY

Then, of course, there is fiction, which, despite relying wholly on creativity, is in the most part based on true life experiences. There is no fiction which does not depend, at least in part, upon truth.

A Mug's Game
Stories

This is a work of fiction, in that the author does not know of it having happened. But it could have, and somewhere, someone will read it and wonder: 'How could he have known about that?'

A Mug's Game

IT wasn't often these days that Archie would have a bet. Mainly he'd just sit on a stool, propped in front of the main screen at the off-course tote shop, and watch. He didn't miss much, but he didn't do much either.

He was a familiar figure and the 'young bucks' who came into the TAB throwing their money around all knew him.

'How yer doin' Archie-boy?' asked 'The Jangler' as he reached for a betting card from the counter in front of him. Jimmy was a regular at the agency but unfortunately had got his nickname from the fact that by the time he left each day, whatever he had in his pockets was much more likely to jangle than to rustle. Often it made no sound at all.

Jimmy's mate, and antithesis, was Rob — deeper and more scholarly — and whose moniker, 'The Rustler', also was appropriate for reasons at the opposite end of the financial scale.

Nevertheless, they were mates, and swapped opinions as they analysed the form together, occasionally asking Archie what he thought, which usually amounted to not much anyway.

'Yer had a bet Arch?' inquired Jimmy, knowing that if he could be as sure of backing a winner as he was of the answer, it would all be very easy indeed.

'Not today, Jim, not today,' Archie replied predictably.

'I'm in no hurry ...'

Archie never was in a hurry either — he'd have a bet occasionally, and usually he'd collect, but, as the boys jokingly told him on a regular basis, you wouldn't want to be holding your breath waiting for it to happen.

'Yer a patient man, Arch, I'll say that for you,' declared Rob with that note of respect which can sometimes be found in those with enough knowledge to recognise talent when they see it.

Jimmy's approach was different.

'Come on Arch,' he'd say, 'I reckon this thing's a moral in the next at Cranbourne — how about we take it with a few in the trifecta and go halves?'

Archie sometimes agreed, but it certainly was not a regular occurrence and if he did, Jimmy got to thinking he must be onto something. Jimmy was never quite sure whether, for once, Archie agreed with his judgment or whether he'd struck an infrequent lapse into boredom and needed 'a fix' to stimulate his punter's brain. All he really knew was that Archie was less likely to need a 'fix' than anyone he'd ever met in a tote. He also reflected that, of all the bets he had, it was the ones they shared which generally were the most productive.

Jimmy and Rob knew nothing much about Archie, except that he seemed to spend most of his time in the TAB, just watching. He seemed like a nice old guy — or 'old' to them anyway — and a pretty good judge when you could nail him down to declaring an opinion, but what they noticed most was his patience.

It was a freezing Melbourne mid-winter's day — storms had swept the state, washing out the races and the trots, but The Jangler and The Rustler were there, with Archie firmly planted on his usual stool.

'Jeez, Arch, this is a pain,' declared Jimmy. 'I really need a decent win and there's nothing worth betting on.'

'So you're still waiting for your big winner to come along, are you?' he asked Archie, mostly for something to say.

The old man paused and for a moment he seemed lost in thought.

'No, son,' he replied, 'I've already had mine,' then, noticing their quizzical looks, added 'but if I told you about it, you wouldn't believe me.'

Jimmy and Rob exchanged glances and a quick look around at the tote screens. There really wasn't much doing.

'We'll believe you Arch,' declared Jimmy, 'and even if we don't, it's still better than going out there,' he added, waving his hand towards the commuters scurrying through the driving rain as they splashed their way across the pedestrian crossing.

Archie paused, as if considering his options.

'Okay,' he said, 'I'll tell you a story, but it won't help you to back a winner today, or next week, or ever, but it would have if you'd been around when it happened.'

Archie paused again and slowly gazed around the TAB agency with all its television screens and prices monitors, self-service machines, computer-generated form guides and all the other 'mod-cons' of the technological age.

'It's all this crap that's buggered it all up,' he announced. 'It used to be fun, a challenge and you used to be able to get a quid if you were smart, but those days are gone.

'I grew up on a farm and Dad had a few mares and I always wanted to be a jockey, but going to Vietnam stuffed that.'

'You two are too young to remember the Vietnam War in the sixties – stupidest war they ever had. We didn't know why we were going and when we got back we didn't know why we'd been, but we went anyway.'

'I don't think we changed Vietnam much, but we changed ourselves a bit, most of us ...'

Archie paused for what seemed a long time, his eyes clouded as his mind whirled back through the mists of another era.

Archie was sitting on the edge of the jungle, shrouded from sight by the canopy of green foliage. He had a clear view in front of him, past the buffalo grass to the paddy fields that formed a patchwork quilt as the land sloped down to the little village in the distance.

It was a good vantage point, they knew that, and it would be almost impossible for anything significant to happen at ground level without them knowing, but what was going on in the maze of underground tunnels on the outskirts of Than Khe was another matter.

Waiting and watching for the Viet Cong was bad enough, but ultimately it was the bloody boredom that would get to you, he reflected. There wasn't much you could do about it, either – you couldn't hoon around and play footy like you could back at the base. All you could do was sit and talk. Watch and wait.

Most of them talked about women – all the bloody time! A few of them had wives and even babies, some had girlfriends and others just had fantasies.

Archie and Eddie talked about women too, but more usually it was horses and tales of 'the punt'. There was plenty of time to think and both of them had fertile minds when it came to dreaming up schemes for that elusive 'racetrack certainty'.

'You know mate,' said Archie one day, 'if we ever get out of this stinkin' place, one day we'll set one up and get enough money to fill a shithouse.'

'Yeah, right,' said Eddie, 'we'll get to all the jocks and fix the friggin' Melbourne Cup.'

'Don't be a smart-arse.'

Archie's tone had changed.

'We won't go anywhere near the Melbourne Cup, but if what I'm thinking about works, and it will work, it'll be just as good.'

'I've got a plan, mate. It'll take a while but there's no risk and it'll only need the two of us to make it work. All we gotta do is get out of this bloody place, keep our traps shut and be patient.'

Archie knew he'd found the right partner to put his scheme into practice.

'All we need is for the bloody dinks to piss off and leave us alone,' he declared.

'Eddie lived in the Barossa Valley in South Australia,' Archie continued, 'and at that stage I lived just outside Melbourne, near Whittlesea.'

The Jangler had lost interest in the price fluctuations for the interstate dogs and The Rustler sat absently drawing arrows on a betting card.

'Eddie's dad had died while he was away, so he'd inherited the farm and all the horses. I bought a few acres and got a couple of second-hand racehorses and a few old broodmares and started breeding a few foals.

'The important part about it was that he was in South Australia and I was in Victoria and all the birth and death notifications had to go to the Registrar in NSW.

'I trained a few winners, nothing special, and just sort of pottered along for the first few years. I'd ring Eddie every now and then. He was always going a bit better than me, mostly coz he had more horses and some of the ones his dad had left him were a bit better class than mine.

'Eddie gradually developed a reputation as a bloke who had his share of success and after a while everyone looked on me as being just a battler, which was fair enough, because that's what I was. I was happy enough with that. I didn't want to be getting a reputation of being a smarty.'

Jimmy was starting to get restless, as he did when he'd been inside a TAB for half an hour without having a bet.

'So what's the big deal?' he demanded, with a sideways glance towards the screen showing the odds for the next at the Cessnock dogs.

Archie paused, making sure he had the attention of his audience, then continued.

'The key to the whole thing,' he explained, glancing over his shoulder to make sure they were out of earshot, 'was that I didn't ever notify the death of one of my mares until they were absolutely too old to breed, but every year I sent in a foal notification for all of them, even the dead ones.'

'You're kidding!' exclaimed The Jangler.

'No,' Archie continued, 'if they actually had a foal, I'd notify it in the normal way, but if they didn't, I'd invent one that was identical to one of Eddie's.'

Rob glanced at Jimmy, who looked like he was in a trance.

'Nobody ever checked,' Archie continued, 'or not until they went to the races anyway, and there wasn't any DNA or blood-typing or lip tattoos or freeze brands or any of that shit in those days – there was just your description of the horse and its brand, which could be as simple or as complicated as you liked.

'Eddie would breed one out of one of his good mares, register it and send me a copy of the papers.

'It might be a bay colt with a white near-hind and a star on its forehead, the kind of markings that were a dime a dozen. He'd brand it with a "T" on the off shoulder, nice simple brand, and it would be registered as, say, by Without Fear from Nulla Belle.

'I'd fill out a notification certificate for a bay colt by one of my own stallions from one of my barren mares, or one of the dead ones. Let's say her name was Entreaty ...'

'Yeah, you wish,' interjected Rob. It surprised Archie, who emerged from the depths of his serious narrative with a smile as he realised The Rustler had 'caught him out' using the name of Phar Lap's dam as his hypothetical example.

The Jangler looked puzzled but neither of his mates deigned to fill him in and Archie resumed his tale.

'Anyway,' he said, 'I'd just fill in everything so it was identical to Eddie's and send off the papers to the Registrar and wait.

'The only thing you had to be a little bit careful about was the whorls," Archie continued. 'You know what a whorl is?' he queried, turning to Jimmy.

Jimmy was becoming even more puzzled. 'Of course I know what a bloody wall is,' he retorted. 'They're used for holding the friggin' roof up,' he added with what he thought was just a touch of sarcasm.

Archie let it pass.

'Not a "W-A-double-L",' he said, 'a "W-H-O-R-L".'

This time Jimmy looked blank, for which The Rustler was grateful. He was pretending to understand but was more than happy to have Archie go into his explanation.

'A whorl,' Archie hesitated, 'is like sort of a circular ridge of hair on a horse's neck or head and no two horses have whorls the same, so they're like fingerprints.

'You have to mark the whorls on the identification papers, but I always used to change them a bit from what Eddie sent me – either leave one out or move them a bit, not enough to look wrong but enough so they weren't quite identical.'

Archie had been very thorough. To register two horses as being exactly identical would have been to invite discovery of the plot had anyone ever become suspicious.

'I probably needn't have bothered,' he continued, 'because the two sets of papers arrived at the Registrar's a few weeks apart from two different states. There weren't any computers, nothing but manual checks, and there was just no way anyone was going to be sitting down comparing the whorls on a horse from one state to the whorls on a horse from somewhere else. Still, I did it, just to be safe.'

Archie looked at his listeners. Jimmy was keeping up and The Rustler's mind had bolted – he probably didn't even need to be told the rest of the story.

'When the time came, Eddie would send in the papers for a racing name and I'd do the same, so what we had in each case was one horse with two identities, one in South Australia and one in Victoria,' Archie went on, 'which was all very well except that the whole thing wasn't worth a pinch of dried goat-shit if he wasn't any good.

'It took a while, I guess it must have been three or four years, then one day Eddie rang me and said: "Mate, I think we've got one".'

Archie knew that one thing they didn't want, so far as the 'sting' was concerned anyway, was a champion. A good horse, yes, a champion, no. Although, he reflected, if they had a champion, maybe that might be a fun way to fill in time while they were waiting for the right one.

They had tried a couple of 'dry runs', with ordinary horses, who were unlikely to attract any attention, and they had worked like a charm.

Eddie gave each horse a few runs under his South Australian name, and then sent him to Archie, who took him to the races under his Victorian name.

The stewards inspected him and checked his papers before his first start in South Australia and satisfied themselves that he was, in fact, say, 'Fearless Song'.

Then, when he came to Victoria, the stewards there checked him out and found that the papers Archie produced for them proved beyond doubt that he was 'Bold Invader'. The color checked out, as did the markings, the brand, the sex, the teeth and, more or less, the whorls. How simple could it be?

On a couple of occasions Eddie won a race or two at the provincials with a horse before he sent it on to Archie, who took it to a country maiden class event, more to test the system than to try to win. Usually, in fact, he made sure they didn't. It was easy enough to lock them in their boxes for a couple of days, drop them off hard feed then give them a big bran mash for breakfast on race morning. If that didn't take the edge off them, nothing would.

Archie resolutely avoided the little temptations: his mind was firmly focused on 'the bigger picture'.

There were a couple of other rules: never engage a 'fashionable' jockey and never give the horse the benefit of an apprentice's claim. If you didn't want them to win, make it as difficult for them as possible.

Archie didn't want to develop a reputation for producing first-up winners. Being low-key and generally unsuccessful was just one of the details which had their parts to play in the background tapestry he was so painstakingly weaving.

Now and then Archie would 'let one go' at an obscure country meeting, or even a picnic fixture, just so it wouldn't come as too great a shock to anyone if one day he produced a handy horse, as struggling trainers occasionally do.

Mostly, though, it was pretty much business as usual. Just about the most exciting thing that ever happened, on the surface anyway, was when Archie would win a race with one of them, then sell it to a rival trainer's client. They usually thought they were getting a bargain and probably were.

It helped pay the expenses and Archie and Eddie would go halves in the proceeds and silently drink to 'the system'. It worked, and both of them knew it!

By the time he'd recounted this part of his story, Archie had emerged from his earlier conspiratorial, sombre countenance to a mood of mildly excited animation – something neither The Jangler nor The Rustler had observed in him before.

'You know what it's like when you really spot one in the form guide and you can't wait for the meeting and for the betting to start?' he asked them, already knowing the answer.

The Jangler's eyes lit up like a kid in a lolly shop.

'Well that's the way it was when Eddie rang me with the news.

'I couldn't get excited at that stage because there was nothing really happening. It was a bit like a kid being told in April that there really is a Santa Claus – pretty good news but it's going to be a long wait, even if it turns out to be right.'

'So what was the hold-up?' queried The Jangler, whose character traits did not include patience. Jimmy definitely did not have the temperament to handle what Archie was about to tell him.

'The hold-up, as you put it, was that so far all we had was Eddie's judgment that we had the right horse – one we were certain was good enough to do the job but not good enough to start attracting attention either from the stewards, the public or anyone else. We didn't want anyone getting excited about him – he didn't need a fan club!'

Archie explained to Jimmy that not everyone needed instant gratification in such matters and that he and Eddie were happy to employ the philosophy of 'slowly, slowly, catchee monkey'. Archie and Rob were not too surprised that The Jangler did not seem to understand, although, talking of monkeys, they were equally sure it wouldn't take much more than a tip from someone who claimed to have a 'good thing' at the monkey races and Jimmy would be off.

As it was, Jimmy took another look at the hailstones piling up against the unprotected shop-fronts and the commuters sheltering, shivering, in doorways and decided he was pretty interested in Archie's story after all.

'At that stage Eddie had only given this colt a couple of gallops but he'd shown him ability and manners and he had a good attitude,' Archie went on.

Eddie had told him on the phone that the colt was an amazingly quick learner and was 'just a natural'.

'You'd swear he'd been here before,' Eddie had said. 'He seems to know it all before you teach him and he remembers everything.'

Archie knew that ones like that, if they could run too, were like gold dust. From what Eddie had told him, the only concern was that the youngster might be too good to fill the bill for what they had in mind, but Eddie was quick to allay his fears.

'Don't worry about that, mate, he knows how to look after himself – he lies down and sleeps most of the day and on the track he does only what he has to, but it doesn't matter what I work him against, he can handle them. He doesn't run away from them – just beats them, every time!'

So Archie had been convinced and set about applying for a racing name for the youngster, now a two-year-old, whose foal-notification papers, lodged the previous year, said he was a black or brown son of Archie's own stallion, Dark Nulla, from Twilight Time. They listed his only white mark as being a small star on his forehead and his brand as 'T' on the off-shoulder.

What Archie knew, but the Registrar didn't, was that Twilight Time had been dead for four years. Her death notification form had been filled out, ready to be posted, and if anyone had ever checked, they would have been told she had 'died last week'.

'It's important to be careful with the genetic color rules,' Archie explained to Jimmy and Rob, 'because if you don't, you could come unstuck.

'If you're just making up who their parents were, like I was, you need to be pretty sharp and do your homework and not get it wrong. You have to stick to the genetic rules.

'For instance, bay is the most dominant color, which explains why there are more bays than any others, and chestnut is the least dominant. That means you can get a bay in just about any circumstances but you can't get a chestnut unless at least one grandparent on each side of their pedigree is chestnut.

'There are genetic rules about breeding greys, too, but we decided we weren't going to have anything to do with greys because they're too conspicuous and that was something we could do without.'

Archie told his now avid disciples that in South Australia the little colt had been notified as being by the Lindsay Park Stud's imported siring sensation Without Fear from a mare by Romantic, appropriately named Romancing. Eddie had at least shown some imagination and applied for the racing name 'Proposal'.

In Victoria, however, the youngster would live his life as the son of Dark Nulla and Twilight Time and would race as 'Promiscuity'.

'Who named him that?' Jimmy demanded of Archie.

'I did.'

'And how the hell did you get a name like that out of his breeding?'

Archie grinned. He was really beginning to enjoy this.

'Well, for a start I reckon old 'Twilight' must have been a bit promiscuous to still be having foals after being dead for four years,' he chuckled, 'and his South Australian parents were Romancing and Without Fear – think about it!

'Anyway, I liked the name,' Archie declared.

'In any case,' said Archie, 'Eddie was pretty right. He rang a few months later and told me he was going terrific but there were a couple of the jocks knew about him from riding him and riding against him in trackwork, so it wasn't much of a secret.

'He took him to Gawler in a Maiden Three-Year-Old and they put their money on him, and a few bob of mine. They got a bit of 10-1 and averaged 8s – I think he started about 4-1.'

'And ...?'

'He shit in – just jumped out, sat outside the leader and won by half a length. The kid said it could have been five; you know I told you he was lazy.'

The Jangler looked disappointed. 'You're not going to tell us that was your big winner? There's got to be more to it than that!'

'Yes mate.' Archie was starting to sound either exasperated or condescending, but The Rustler couldn't work out which. 'That was the first step along The Yellow Brick Road – you know, the road that was paved with gold ...'

Archie was enjoying himself. He'd never told anyone any of this before and probably hadn't expected that he ever would. He had a couple of willing listeners, though, and they were knockabout punters who understood everything he said (well, Rob did anyway, but he wasn't too sure about Jimmy). In any case, it didn't matter anymore – Eddie was gone, most of the bookies were long dead and all he had to remind him of Promiscuity were a couple of photos and the grave with its headstone in the lower paddock, down by the river. And then, of course, there was the money ...

Archie recounted how Eddie had allowed Proposal to win his way through his classes on the provincial tracks around Adelaide before taking him to a better class fixture at one of the metropolitan tracks, Cheltenham.

'He was going for his fourth win on end but it rained all the previous night and the track was a bog,' he recalled.

'Eddie wasn't sure how he'd handle the ground so he just said to the jockey: 'Stay out of trouble, look after him and win if you have to.'

'Well, he handled it and the others didn't and it didn't matter that he was bone lazy, he still won, not by much, but with a bit in hand.

'All that really did was tell us what we needed to know, that he could handle the wet if he had to, and that it was just about time to go. We needed to talk and you never know when some bastard's going to tap a trainer or a jockey's phone, especially if he's a bit successful, so we decided that I'd better go over for the Anzac Day march in Adelaide.

'It was good, too. We caught up with a few of the other guys, had a few beers, told a few lies then went back to Eddie's for dinner. I would have liked to have stayed but I didn't want his stable guys seeing me there when they arrived for work in the morning.

'Anyway, he introduced me to Proposal – he was a beautiful, strong-looking colt, that close to black it didn't matter – then we had a long talk and made a few plans.'

Archie reflected for a moment. His thoughts drifted to a day nearly 30 years earlier. He was reading The Sporting Globe, scanning the race weights for Australia's biggest provincial race carnival, the May meeting at Warrnambool. There, in the entries for the Maiden Three-Year-Old on the third day, was Promiscuity.

'The only way you're ever going to get much money out of the bookies,' Archie continued conspiratorially, 'is if you know something they don't and in this business it's pretty easy for the cat to get out of the bag.'

'Yeah, and pretty hard to get him back in again,' grinned The Rustler.

The Rustler was a 'value man' – he loved backing 50-1 shots he thought should be 5-1 – but he knew it didn't take much, like an eye-catching run, for today's 50-1 shot to open up favourite in the betting the next time.

He'd also been around racecourses for long enough to know that it didn't take one dollar to shorten a horse's price; all it took was a 'whisper', or for the horse to open at a shorter price than expected on the tote, or for one of the 'smarties' to spot the trainer's wife at a tote window and 'smell a rat'.

Rob knew he didn't need to tell Archie any of this. It was pretty obvious Archie already knew.

'What I'm saying,' Archie continued, 'is that you have to assume you're only going to get one chance, and, if you're going to have a real go, you probably can't afford more than one anyway. So if you're going to do it, you've got to do it right. No stuff ups!'

The jaw set as he looked from Jimmy to The Rustler. He didn't say: 'Right...?' but that's what he meant. This was a side of Archie they hadn't seen before. They knew no response was required and they were beginning to realise that when Archie set his mind to do something, it would take a bloody good man to stop him.

'We picked Warrnambool because that's where the most money is, not all the time, but it definitely is at the May meeting every year,' he said.

'It's like a mini-Melbourne Cup carnival – everyone gets there, all the bookies, all the professional punters and all the landed gentry from round the joint who've got too much money and no bloody idea.

'You'll find occasionally one of the Melbourne trainers will bring one down and try to set it up for a first-up go but usually it's only the country-class horses and they're pretty ordinary.

'The thing about it is that if you've got the best horse and you know he's the best, you don't have to worry too much about the opposition – all you have to worry about is attention to detail and making sure you do your part of it right.

'Eddie and I had waited a long time and we sure as hell weren't going to fuck it up.'

Archie remembered the night he'd set out on the journey. Keyed up? Yeah, he thought, a bit like when they'd left for Vietnam, but jeez, compared to that, this was a breeze.

They'd hooked up the double-float and loaded old Further Ado – he had no hope, but it looked better if you had two – and headed for Horsham. A bit out of the way, but it suited him and it suited Eddie. It wasn't halfway, but it was close. He could get a couple of boxes at the Showgrounds and no-one was likely to notice that he'd arrived with one horse and left next morning with two. The very worst that could happen was that one of the old trotting blokes might come down to check on his horses on the way home from the pub, but that wasn't likely to be a problem, even if it happened.

He was glad of Josie's company. It was better if you had someone to talk to, made the trip go quicker.

Ah, Josie. He remembered when she first came to work for him. Pretty, perky, cheeky little Josie, with the red hair and the 'soft' hands that made horses run. Josie – as tough as an iron fist in a velvet glove.

He smiled to himself as he remembered her first few race rides. Some of the jocks seemed to delude themselves that if they did her a favor on the track she might do them one 'off the track'. Fat chance! That was before they found out she'd bite their bloody balls off if they got in the way. Yeah, she was a stunner, Josie, but boy, could she ride!

He hadn't told her, only that they were going to Horsham overnight to pick up a horse they'd be taking home after he raced at Warrnambool. But it wouldn't have mattered if he had, he could trust her, he knew that. All Josie was interested in was riding – the more rides the better.

A few trainers were starting to respect her ability and give her a ride or two, especially when she could take her five pounds 'claim' and get a bit of weight off their horses' backs. A dozen winners in an apprentice's first twelve months was a pretty good effort and people were starting to notice.

Still, she wasn't 'fashionable' yet and Archie knew no-one would take any notice of her engagement to ride Promiscuity. She had plenty going for her – the five pound claim was just one more factor in their favor, and she'd do as she was told. She'd ride him as well as any of them.

'The Showgrounds was a good place to meet and I'd organised a couple of boxes away from the other horses who lived there,' Archie explained. 'I told the bloke on the phone that I had a colt and that he could be a bit rowdy, so that was sweet and it suited us too.

'Eddie lobbed at about nine o'clock and Proposal walked off the float and, lo-and-behold, he turned into Promiscuity.'

The Jangler had totally lost interest in the Cessnock dogs and The Rustler was having an adrenalin rush.

'We got going before the trotting blokes arrived in the morning,' said Archie, 'and when we got to Warrnambool everyone at the stables where we were staying was running around getting ready for the races.

'Josie had a couple of rides, which was good because she hadn't ridden there before and it gave her a chance to have a look at the track, not that she needed to, but it made me feel better.

'That was the Wednesday and ours were in on the Thursday, both of them,' he said.

'I didn't reckon we needed any luck, but we got a bit anyway,' Archie continued. 'Promiscuity was in race five, right in the middle of the program, and drew barrier five.

'The barrier's not that important if you've got a real 'good thing' but you're still better off not drawing in too close, just in case they all want to lead and you've got to kick up to keep from being boxed in. If you're good enough you can always sit outside them – you just have to stay out of trouble.

'The other thing that really worked in our favor was that it had only been a couple of weeks since he'd had a run and I hadn't had to take him home and maybe upset his routine or let anyone see him. Eddie had kept him up to the mark and nobody except Josie knew I hadn't had him all his life. Anyway, no-one would have thought anything of me getting a new horse, even if they'd noticed.

'There were a couple of other details, too,' Archie said, 'just little things that help.'

'It was a bonus having the right kind of race on the third day of the carnival. The Thursday is Cup day and Grand Annual Steeple day and if there's one big day in country racing in Victoria, that's it.'

Archie realised he didn't know why he was telling them that. Rob would already know and, as far as Jimmy was concerned, the fifth at Warrnambool or at Cessnock dogs were about the same as the Melbourne Cup – they were something to bet on – and he really didn't care.

It had been close to 30 years but it seemed like yesterday to Archie as it all came flooding back.

If anyone had asked him, he would have told them he didn't get nervous, not about anything, but he'd found himself tossing and turning all night, going over and over the race in his mind. Eventually he wasn't sure if he'd been awake thinking about it or asleep dreaming about it.

He remembered looking at his watch and not being able to believe it was only half an hour since he'd looked at it last time. It must be wrong! He pulled back the curtain and looked out into the night. Can't get up yet. Christ, even the bloody horse wouldn't be awake!

Eventually daylight came and it felt better once he was going through the race-day routine. Josie was her usual bright little self. *She'd* slept all right. Thank God for that.

Then the trip down the town. Even at the time he'd grinned to himself. He'd told them he was going for a paper, "for the form-guide," he'd said, but had found himself looking for a phone-box instead of a newspaper shop.

Eddie had picked the quaver in his voice. 'Stop worrying, Arch,' he'd said, 'it will be okay – just you do your bit right.'

He knew Eddie wasn't worried, about the horse or him. Eddie knew his professionalism would kick in and that he never made mistakes when it was important. Neither of them would have got home from 'Nam if he had.

Eddie was going to the races at Cheltenham – he'd entered a couple of horses to have an excuse for being there. He had some of the money because there were at least a couple of bookies in the interstate betting ring who didn't mind taking a decent bet. He wouldn't do the business himself – that might look a bit 'suss' – but he'd fix it. Eddie's brother was going to the races in Sydney. Eddie had said he could be trusted and wouldn't ask questions, so that was good enough for Archie.

The form-guide had given him heart. There was an odds-on shot in the race and Promiscuity was listed at 50-1.

'There were a couple of others from Melbourne stables and they'd run placings but were nothing special and I knew the favourite was no star,' Archie continued. 'He'd had about 10 runs and been in the money in most of them but he just couldn't get to the line. He didn't worry me and all the others had had a couple of runs so we knew we weren't running against the new Phar Lap.'

The Rustler was still doodling on the betting card but Archie noticed that now he was drawing dollar signs instead of arrows.

'From there on it was just a matter of going through the motions,' Archie said. 'I had to get him inspected, you know, his brands and everything, but that was no problem because all his markings tallied with his foal notification papers, didn't they?' Archie checked that his listeners were keeping up.

'Joffa, the bloke I was stabled with, was an old bush trainer who I knew could keep his trap shut, so I told him I needed a hand with a little job and asked him if he could bring a couple of mates and meet me at the bar near the mounting yard after I'd legged Josie on.

'I couldn't give him the money in the bar, so I gave it to him in a paper bag while everyone else was watching the previous race.'

Archie would remember the look on Joffa's face for as long as he lived.

'Put that in your jacket,' he'd said as he handed Joffa something which looked like his lunch. There's six there ... two each.'

'Six hundred,' Joffa had repeated, confirming the figure.

'Six grand ...'

'*Fuck* ...!'

'I'd done my homework. I knew which were the good bookies who'd take a big bet and I told Joffa he and the other blokes should take two each. I kept the couple of biggest ones for myself because I had twice as much as the others and I wanted to get it all on in as few bets as we could.

'I had my wife, my late wife, having a grand on him on the tote on my phone account but it had to be late so as not to give the game away.

'She nearly had a bloody heart-attack when I told her,' he chuckled.

'She was never really a racing person but if she didn't think I knew what I was doing she wouldn't have married me, would she?'

Archie borrowed one of Joffa's strappers to lead Promiscuity into the mounting yard. Eddie had told him the colt wouldn't really take any interest until he went into the barrier stalls and so far he'd proved spot on. He waited for Josie.

Josie and the rest of the jockeys emerged from the scales room sharing little jokes among themselves before splitting and finding their respective groups, most of them made up of a trainer and two or three hopeful owners, including several ladies dressed in anticipation of the trophy presentation after the race.

'What's doing boss?" asked Josie. She already knew that something was doing. She'd worked with Archie for long enough to be able to read his body language.

'This goes all right,' Archie began.

Josie knew she was right.

'I want you to jump him out and go forward. If you land in front or outside the leader, that's great. If they all want to go mad, let them sort themselves out then slide around and either sit outside the lead or go to the front if it's there. Sit three wide if you have to. All you have to do is stay out of trouble. You'll find he's got a bit on them.'

The strapper brought Promiscuity over and Archie legged her up.

He continued to walk with the horse and Josie leaned forward to listen.

'Don't win too easily; we want to leave some for next time. Just win. This is important.'

'Shit!' thought Josie, but said nothing. She'd had plenty of rides for Archie, but he'd never said anything like that before!

'I collected Joffa and his mates from the bar and we spread out. I'd told them to watch me and wait for the signal,' Archie continued.

'I had a hat and told them not to move until I put it on. We'd decided to ask each bookie to bet us the odds to $10,000 but to take whatever they'd bet us. It had been a pretty good betting race; there'd been good money for four or five of them and not two-bob for the colt, so he'd drifted right out and he was 50-1 and 66-1 everywhere.

'That was good enough because he wasn't going to get any better than that and we had to give ourselves time to get it all on. I put my hat on and away we went.

'I had four grand and my first bet was $200 at 50-1, to win $10,000. I asked the second bloke for $20,000 to $300 at 66-1 but he'd only bet me half, $10,000 to $150.

'They both turned him down to 25s but I got another $10,000 to $400 from both of them.

'I got most of the rest of mine on at 50s and 40s before they realised what was going on and by the time they did, it didn't matter because we'd finished anyway and they were going into the barrier. We averaged just under 40-1.

'What you've got to remember was this was 30 years ago. You could buy a pretty good house for not much more than $10,000.'

There were only a couple left to go into the stalls when Archie found a vantage point on the lawn in front of the grandstand. By the time he had his binoculars focused, they were all in and ready to go.

Archie felt sick. Fear. The same sort of sick he'd felt in those moments suspended in time in Vietnam. Fear of the unknown. A lack of control. Waiting for your life to happen, knowing you'd put yourself in a position and you could no longer change it.

'Fuck you, Archie,' he thought, 'it's only a race – it's only money …' His crotch tingled and he found himself taking a long, deep breath.

His life seemed to be passing in slow motion. In an instant, but gradually, cold panic transcended into the warmth of confidence. Still he held his breath, but now he was ready.

'Racing …' called the course broadcaster, 'and they're away in a good line …'

Archie searched for the black and white colors and the red cap with its pom-pom. Josie loved the pom-pom and it made the colors easy to find, even in a bunched field.

This one was bunched as they raced through the first furlong, but the pom-pom was there in the leading group, on the outside, a couple of lengths off the front.

Archie could feel his whole life happening in the moment, but the panic had gone and he felt in control. The binoculars wouldn't quite stay still, but that was okay, he could live with that.

It was all unfolding. The leaders were going hard and were beginning to string out, the ones caught wide starting to drop into positions nearer the inside rail. The colt was three wide, sliding around them with Josie crouched low as he strode up to get to the leader's girth.

Archie had thought he had learned the colors of the other main contenders – he liked to know what was going on in a race – but now he could see only one horse.

The commentator's voice was rising as they neared the home turn, but Archie was oblivious to it, except for the echo of 'Promiscuity …' somewhere in his sub-conscious, far-off, as in a dream.

'Whoa boy, whoa … easy boy …' Josie's voice was soothing. Promiscuity was striding freely, edging closer to the leader.

Josie had been talking to the colt since they'd got to the barrier stalls.

'You're a good boy, aren't you ...?' she'd said, stroking his neck as they waited for the last few of his opponents to be loaded.

Now they were rounding the turn, about to straighten for the run to the line and she felt like she was driving a Rolls-Royce.

'Just sit,' she told herself, 'not yet ...'

The jockey on the leader was roaring at him and behind her she could hear the yelling, the pounding hooves and the thwack of the whips.

Promiscuity was outside the leader, a neck behind and flicking his ears. Underneath her he felt like a coiled spring.

She thought about taking a glance over her shoulder. 'Never look back,' she'd been told, so she didn't.

She had the leader covered, she knew that, and there was nothing close behind; despite the roar of the crowd, you could tell from the sounds.

'Be professional!' the voice in her head told her. 'Don't get too cute!' She knew she could have been four lengths in front, but Archie had told her not to win too easily. 'Just win,' he'd said. It rang in her ears.

They were inside the final furlong. 'Come on, mate!' she yelled at the colt and gave him a smack down the shoulder with the whip. He felt like he had overdrive.

Suddenly Josie was aware of another presence. On the outside, wide out. Closing.

She couldn't see anything out of the corner of her eye, but she didn't need to be able to see.

In a flash she was riding for her life and the colt flattened out as the whip stung him and he surged underneath her.

Now she could see the other horse's head.

Everything was slow motion. She was riding desperately, in perfect rhythm with the colt's stride, but the other head was gaining on them at every bound.

She didn't need to look where the post was, she could feel it. The computer in her mind was calculating how far it was, and how fast the other horse was coming.

They hit the line. Josie thought she'd won. In close photos you were nearly always right. Usually you knew. But not always.

Josie looked across. First she saw the horse's nose, then gradually her perception took in the head, then the neck and the flapping reins, then the saddle. The saddle. There was no-one there.

The riderless horse careered on as Josie put the whip away and adjusted her grip on the reins.

'He won by four lengths,' Archie said, 'and we never did get a decent price about him again.

'Still, I bought the farm and the block of flats and they've given me a pretty nice income over the years. I've never had to worry too much since then. There's still a bit in the bank, so I can't complain.

'There were a few mumbles about him being a ring-in, of course, mainly from a couple of the bookies, but the stewards checked him against his papers again and there were never going to be any worries.

'They say the punt's a mug's game and I guess mostly they're right. But I suppose it depends on whether it's you that's the mug.'

The rain had eased outside and it was starting to get dark. The guy behind the counter was tidying up. A couple of the desperates were peering at the race lists for the last at Cessnock dogs.

'You had enough mate?' The Rustler asked The Jangler.

Archie looked at his watch. 'Well, I'd better get going,' he said.

'Josie'll have my tea ready. I'll see you fellas tomorrow ...'

The Feast Of Stephen
Stories

Written in 2003, this story is 'creative non-fiction', in that it is based in part upon events which actually occurred.

The Feast Of Stephen

> *'Good King Wenceslas looked out, on the Feast of Stephen,*
> *Where the snow lay all about, deep and crisp and even ...'*

THE words ran involuntarily through Susan's mind as she worked behind the desk. She liked Christmas with its festivity and carols although she'd seen enough Christmases to be a touch sceptical about the 'peace on Earth and goodwill to Men' bit.

Not that she'd thought much about it, nor about the tune; it was just there, somewhere in the background – she wasn't even aware she was 'singing along'. Occasionally Susan's subconscious would wince, but she was preoccupied with what she was doing and didn't really notice.

The squeak of the clarinet reed betrayed the amateur status of its player.

But the coins in the cardboard box on the ground in front of his little brother, seated on the footpath beside him, indicated he was a professional, if not in the true sense of the word. And the tortured squeals of his sister's flute suggested it was, indeed, a family concern.

The young girl pursed her lips and concentrated, but 'Good King Wenceslas' still didn't sound much like it did over the sound systems in all the big shopping centres.

But maybe it didn't matter quite so much here in Jarvis Street, away from the hustle and bustle of the shoppers and their frantic last minute Christmas spendfest.

Life seemed more tranquil here, in its way, and most of the pedestrians – some bleary-eyed, some colourful and animated – seemed not to notice. Jarvis Street was like that: you could sit at a pavement coffee table and see anyone from Hopalong Cassidy to Van Gogh to The Wicked Witch of the West pass by within a matter of minutes. Outside coffee tables in Jarvis Street weren't for drinking coffee; they were for entertainment in watching the passing parade.

Occasionally the musicians struck a note of harmony and, admittedly, the tunes were identifiable. But, after all, it was Christmas, and they were Christmas songs, which sometimes provided the principal clue.

Their little brother, sitting on what looked like a neatly folded cardigan, seemed oblivious to what was going on around him and quite happy to play with the modest collection of coins the day's efforts had produced. There had been a five dollar note at one stage, thrown in by one of the desperates who frequented the betting shop just along the street. It seemed he'd struck it lucky and hadn't walked far enough for the elation, combined with his momentary attack of 'the spirit of Christmas', to dissipate. A few minutes later he'd be wondering what he'd been thinking about, giving away the cost of a pot of beer, but Christmas did funny things to people.

The boy had 'abandoned his post' – leaving 'Silent Night' as a flute solo – for long enough to grab the note, plus a few of the coins, and stuff them in his pocket. After all, leaving a banknote visible in Jarvis Street definitely wasn't a good idea and having too much money in the box robbed you of the sympathy vote.

The boy's clarinet had seen better days. The couple of strategically placed pieces of black tape emphasised the point and a close inspection of the pads, which are supposed to open and close the holes when their various keys are depressed, revealed that perhaps it was the instrument which was mainly responsible for some of the abrasive notes emanating from it, rather than a lack of expertise on his part. Still, he was never going to be Benny Goodman, and it could only be hoped he never tackled 'The Golden Wedding'.

Nevertheless, there was no doubt the boy's musical interest and ability, such as it was, was genetic. His father, Michael, had never wanted to do anything else and music had been his life for as long as he could remember. He'd learned on the school's instruments and Mr Overton had recognised his talent and given him extra tuition after school and allowed him to take home one of the old clarinets which hadn't been out of the storeroom in the previous decade. He absorbed the music like a sponge and spent most weekends 'jamming' with Ritchie and Johnny. They called themselves 'The Three Wise Men', not because of any particular wisdom, or manhood for that matter – or not at that stage anyway – but because it was during the Christmas holidays and the name seemed obvious.

Their first gig was in a little restaurant on the outskirts of the city and what they were paid barely covered their train fares getting there. It had been supposed to be a 'one night stand', but they'd made an impression and the owner had asked them first if they wanted to do one night a week, and later the four main nights, from Thursday to Sunday. Michael had loved the work but by that time he was doing an electrical apprenticeship during the day and spent most of the weekend trying to recover from Thursday and Friday.

He found the little white pills gave him a lift and helped him get through. And they added another dimension to the music, a crispness and individuality.

'The Rotten Rodent' was pretty much as its name implied – sleazy and smoky and murky – but it had a cult status and was always packed. The clientele was very different to that of the restaurant, but so was the money, which was the reason for the move. Michael found his day job arduous and boring and started missing days, so wasn't too surprised when the boss told him to collect his pay and not come back. Still, he had more money now and, working at The Rotten Rodent, pot was a way of life and anything further up the scale was simply a matter of choice. There was speed, or crack, or coke or ecstasy, whatever you wanted – it was like a supermarket!

He was sceptical when Sergio, the proprietor, told them the band needed a singer, but one look at Rosa convinced him they needed her, whether she could sing or not.

Their first son was born the day after Christmas Day, on December 26. To most people it was Boxing Day, but to Rosa it was St. Stephen's Day. Her religious upbringing had long been cast astern, but she remembered the saints' days and particularly The Feast of Stephen. It seemed like a good name for a son.

Rosa had continued singing with the band, almost uninterrupted by her pregnancy and Stephen's birth, but when Natalie was born she decided she had to have a break, at least until the two were old enough to be left confidently in the care of a babysitter. Good babysitters were hard to find, and you certainly didn't find them at The Rotten Rodent.

It didn't take Sergio long to work out that 'The Three Wise Men' were not quite the attraction that 'Rosa and The Three Wise Men' had been and he'd been thinking for a while it was time for a change.

It wasn't so bad for Johnny and Ritchie – they had homes to go to and didn't have to feed a family. And there was the accessibility to the pills, which Michael found he needed these days just to get out of bed, let alone to perform all night. He could still find them, but it had been easier at 'The Rodent' – there it wasn't a matter of you finding them; they found you.

Rosa had stuck it out for years, watching Michael destroy himself, but had done a lot of thinking during the months leading up to Christian's birth. She would have preferred discussion, and that any decision had been a mutual one, but Michael was never one for 'deep and meaningfuls'. Her attempts to talk were always nipped in the bud and it seemed Michael was, if not content, at least resigned to the gradual slide in their lives. The band had folded but he was a good muso and still got the occasional job, although these days mostly they survived on his session work.

It wasn't that he hadn't tried, she had to admit that. He obviously loved his kids and had done his best to instil his love of music in them, teaching them to play the variety of instruments, in various states of repair, to be found about the house. His 'work instruments' were always cleaned and put away, whatever state he was in, but once they were finished, they were finished. There had been one occasion, when he was 'between jobs', he had tried to hock the old ones, but the pawnbroker wasn't interested, so Michael had given them to the kids.

When Rosa came out of hospital with Christian, it was not to the house she had shared with Michael for seven years. She wondered how she'd lasted as long as she had, but the answer was simple: she loved him ... still did. But it wasn't enough.

For a start it had been a real struggle, on the dole with rent to pay and three kids to feed, but Rosa had battled through, doing cleaning jobs that paid cash and later, when Christian was old enough to be left at home at night in the care of the others, earning extra dollars in a club where she sang, danced with the 'gentlemen' and sat on their laps but refused the lucrative offers for 'extra services' which most of the girls accepted to provide themselves with a higher standard of living.

Rosa hated that part of it, but she loved the singing and allowed herself to fantasise that one night a famous record producer would walk through the door and 'discover' her. It didn't happen, but the thought provided her with hope, which otherwise was in short supply.

It was the kids' idea. Occasionally, when they'd walked through the shopping centre, they had seen buskers on the footpath, performing for the coins people would throw at their feet.

'Can we do that, Mummy?' Natalie has asked one day, as they passed a scruffy young man playing a violin. 'Stephen and I could do that …'

Rosa's response was cut short by Stephen's 'Yeah, Mum, can we …?'

'We'll see,' said Rosa, buying time to think. 'Ask me tomorrow.'

Rosa had awoken to the shriek of the split reed of a clarinet, then became aware of 'Jingle Bells' being played on a piccolo. It was Sunday morning and she'd got home from the club at 4am. She squinted at the bedside clock. It was 6:11.

Her immediate reaction was to storm into the other room and scream at them, but she lay for a moment, listening.

There weren't many squeaks, especially considering the instruments, and at least it was good enough for her to recognise the tune.

It was during 'Silent Night' Rosa made her decision.

'Listen, you two,' she said from the doorway. 'Mummy's very tired and Mrs Keating will be banging on the wall in a minute. Now go back to bed, and you can practice after breakfast.'

Rosa got another couple of hours sleep before she was aware of Natalie touching her arm.

'I've brought you a cup of tea, Mummy,' she said.

When Rosa walked wearily into the kitchen ten minutes later she found Christian, Vegemite from one end of him to the other, eating toast, while Stephen and Natalie stood in front of the music stand, instruments in hand, fingering but not blowing.

'Mummy can we practice now?' asked Natalie. 'We've had our breakfast.'

Rosa cleaned up Christian and went shopping, leaving the musicians to their practice. It was Christmas next week, and Stephen's birthday, and the budget was tight. Of all the times you could be born, she'd often thought, Christmas was probably the worst. After all, who was going to give anyone two gifts when one would do?

Her first stop was the music store. She'd known the proprietor for years, but hadn't been there since before Christian was born.

'Hi Julian,' she greeted him with a wide smile.

'Hello Rosa,' he beamed, 'It's great to see you. Merry Christmas.'

'And to you too.'

'It's been a long time. How are you ...?'

'I'm fine,' she said, not really believing it.

'And what can I do for you?'

'I'd like a couple of clarinet reeds if you've got some.'

'Sure,' he replied. Then, quizzically, 'are you back with Michael?'

'No, no, nothing like that. They're for Stephen.'

Rosa knew Jarvis Street wasn't the best venue to start a career, but she also knew if they were going to collect any money for their efforts, that, short of taking them into the city, it was the only place to be. She thought about where would be safest and decided they were less likely to be harassed outside the Medical Clinic than most places.

She was hesitant at first about leaving Christian with them, but he couldn't be left at home by himself and Rosa was streetwise enough to know there was a certain value to having a little kid sitting beside the collection box, even in Jarvis Street.

She watched them set up and listened to their renditions of 'Silent Night' and 'Jingle Bells', giving a little round of solo applause after each one. She had a cleaning job to go to, but she had to be sure they were okay.

'We'll be all right now, Mummy,' Natalie assured her after the second song. 'Will you come and get us ...?'

'Of course I'll come and get you, Sweetheart. I'll bring you some lunch a bit later and see how you're going.'

Rosa set off across the street but took cover behind a delivery truck where she could see them without them seeing her. They had been through their three-song repertoire three times by the time she set off. They weren't very good, she thought, but they weren't that bad, either. Benny Goodman himself would be battling to make that clarinet sound pure.

Stephen and Natalie had decided that for the first day they should stick to the three songs they knew best, so the sounds of 'Silent Night', 'Jingle Bells' and 'Good King Wenceslas', on clarinet and flute, or occasionally clarinet and piccolo, washed over the mish-mash of humanity who saunter or bustle or glide or shuffle along Jarvis Street in the days before Christmas.

Occasionally an old lady, or a drunk, or a junkie would stop to talk to them between renditions, some dropping a coin or two in Christian's cardboard box, but most passing by, either oblivious or pretending to be. The occasional squeaks and shrieks didn't seem to bother the passing parade, which wasn't too surprising – just a few more hazy sounds in a mostly hazy world.

Margaret sensed Susan was becoming progressively more agitated behind the desk at the Medical Clinic. They worked together a lot and it wasn't like her. She was usually so cool and unflappable.

'How much do you think we'd have to pay them to go away?' demanded Susan suddenly. 'If I hear "Jingle Bells" one more time I am going to scream.'

'We could take up a collection ...' Margaret ventured with a half-grin, scanning the waiting room for additional contributors. Her reply tailed off as she was distracted by the ringing of the phone.

Neither of them saw the striking, dark-haired woman as she approached the children.

'How's it going, Sweetie?' smiled Rosa to her daughter. 'Here's some lunch for you ...'

'We're getting lots of money, Mummy. Stephen's got a five dollar note! What do you want for Christmas ...?'

The Race Stories

Written in 2002, this story must be classified as 'creative non-fiction' in that not all of it is true. But it could have happened and almost all of it did. The names have not been changed.

The Race

'ON YOUR MARKS!' commanded the starter.

A hush fell over the stadium.

It had come to this. This moment. The focus of my life. The hours, the sweat, the toil, the money, the sacrifices. It had come to this.

It had started in the schoolyard at Murchison the day I raced Jimmy Tweddle.

Mr Milvain, the teacher, was casting the school play. It was about the Trojan War and how Pheidippides had run from the Battle of Marathon to Sparta with news of victory over the invading Persian army. It was important that the best runner in the school play the part of Pheidippides and no-one was sure whether that was Jimmy Tweddle or me. Except me, of course. I was sure.

Not that whoever played Pheidippides was going to have to do any more than jog across the stage carrying what was supposed to be the Olympic torch. He certainly wasn't going to have to sprint the length of the schoolyard and crash into the old wooden fence like I had to do to be sure no-one could say I hadn't beaten Jimmy Tweddle fair and square. And he certainly wasn't going to have to run the 140 miles Pheidippides did, nor even the classic marathon distance of 26 miles and 385 yards so many glory-driven Olympic athletes have done since. But it had to be done properly, nevertheless.

I ran a marathon once. I guess for me that was the beginning of the real running, but before the serious stuff started. Before I was told I had 'potential' and that I should be doing other things.

I don't remember the whole of the marathon, but bits of it seem like yesterday. Like catching the train at 3.30am to take us to the start (because it was a one-way course, as opposed to 'out-and-back'). The carriage-full of bleary-eyed, weirdly-dressed, diverse specimens of humanity, smelling of liniment, smeared with Vaseline and mostly looking like they'd just been evicted from their St Vincent de Paul clothing collection bins.

I remember standing in the middle of 8,000 like-minded idiots, wearing a large plastic garbage bag upside-down over my running gear, head and arms sticking out of the pre-cut holes, waiting in the cold for the 7am start.

Then the race. Turning into Beach Road and the headwind hitting us in the face. God, was it going to be like this for the last 34 kilometres? This bloke running with the group of about ten of us, dashing into a beach-front milk bar, catching up again a couple of minutes later and passing around jelly-beans. Then later someone else disappearing into another shop and coming out with a bag of icy poles. Sweaty runners taking a bite and handing them on to whoever was running beside them.

Then the pain, the jolting, searing, all-over aching pain and 'the wall' that marathon runners talk about, which you think is a load of bull until you hit it.

I remember the endless road, stretching as far ahead as you're brave enough to look. You fix your eyes on a building far, far in the distance and every time you look up to check, it doesn't seem to be any closer, until suddenly you look and it's gone, it's behind you.

And there's the 'rush' (they say it's the release of the body's endorphins), 'the runner's high'. The mind senses the finishing line and the body lifts and the legs begin to stride at a rate which, at that stage, should be impossible. The exhilaration. There's not another feeling like it in the world.

A marathon is not about running a race, or about finishing positions, or even time. It is about aloneness within a herd and single-minded determination to do something that makes no sense. It is about being in one distinct group of people on the planet as opposed to the other group. Being one of those who have gone the distance, and understand what it's about, as opposed to those who haven't, and to whom it cannot possibly be explained.

Running a marathon is about experiencing something unique in life!

That was a long time ago. Firmly in the past, in the 'OUT' basket — done. These days I run only one lap of the track, seldom less, never more. The firm, rubberised, leg-friendly, brick-colored road to nowhere, each lane precise between its two white lines, measured, exact.

The transition took ages, valuable years, transforming 'slow-twitch' fibres to 'fast-twitch'. From plod to power. The 'twitch' fibres in your muscles are what you're born with — 'fast' for speed, 'slow' for endurance — and undoubtedly mine were fast-twitch in the first place. No doubt, in retrospect, I should have stuck to sprinting. But my mind made my legs run a marathon and they lost their zing.

The whole process would have been a lot easier and more sensible without the marathon. A more natural progression. From sprinting across the school yard to sprinting around a track. Simple. Except for the mind part, the experience. Except for the memories and the pride. The *understanding*. The road I'd taken made no sense but I wouldn't have had it any other way.

The road back, from 'slow' to 'fast', was one of frustration. Torn muscles, pulled ligaments, aching legs. Perhaps a pure-bred sprinter might have given up. But a marathon runner — never!

The sessions and their variety were endless. Speed sessions, strength sessions, rhythm, technique, lactic sessions, gym, pool, recovery sessions, drills, repetitions, stretching, time trials, motivation, speed-endurance sessions.

And gradually it all returned. The speed, the purity of technique, the endurance under pressure. Gradually the body adapted — the legs learned about speed and power, the body about grace and poise, the mind about fine-tuning, the persona about care and nurturing, the brain about time, precision, rhythm. The athlete learned to run fast. The body learned to relax at high speed. To flow.

I already knew how to compete, to be competitive. Had I been any other way I would not have hit the school fence so hard the day I beat Jimmy Tweddle. I hadn't needed to, as it turned out, but I hadn't known that at the time. I couldn't take that risk. Not then, not now. Getting beaten didn't bear thinking about. It happened, of course, but if you'd done your best and knew it, you hadn't been beaten at all.

Courage, I'd always thought, went hand in hand with self-discipline. I wasn't sure that was how others saw it, but that was the way I saw it, which was all that mattered to me. I knew self-discipline could be learned but I wasn't so sure about courage. Maybe you had to be born with it. But nothing was ever won by courage alone. Success, in sport anyway, was more about iron will, guts and wanting something badly enough.

And I knew, as I settled on my blocks, that I wanted it badly enough.

I knew that Walter Bauer was in the lane next to me. Walter Bauer who had driven me, asleep in his bed in Germany, as I reeled off rep after rep, alone in the wind and scudding, icy rain, through the long winter months at the training track. Walter Bauer, who had beaten me the only time we'd met in a race.

Only I knew the part Walter Bauer played in my training, and in my life.

'Where are you now, Walter Bauer?' the voice in my head would ask as I rounded the last bend and the wind and the sleet hit me straight in the face.

'You're at home in your bed and I'm training and you're not ... I'm gaining on you Walter Bauer!' the voice would proclaim as I found myself gritting my teeth.

'Relax ... relax ...' the voice would tell me, 'hold your stride, use your arms, run to the line.'

It wasn't *all* Walter Bauer, but on those days when the wind and the rain bit into my flesh and every muscle and sinew screamed in pain, he was always there, a hundred metres from the line. He was *always* there.

And now it had come to this.

I took a deep breath and gently leaned forward, shoulders above my hands, fingers spread, bridged behind the freshly-painted white line glistening against the brick-red track.

Briefly, my gaze followed the curving line of my lane to where the first flight of hurdles gleamed black-and-white in the summer sun.

Slowly, I lowered my eyes and dropped my head.

I waited ...

'SET!'

FOOTNOTE:
At the time of writing, in 2005, Trembath and Bauer had not raced against each other again.

Bauer had won the 400 metres hurdles in the Men's 55-59 age-group at the World Veterans' Athletics Championships in Durban, South Africa, in 1997, with Trembath third.
In the World Rankings in 2003, Trembath was listed at No 1 and Bauer No 6.

They raced each other again only once, in the World Championships final in Riccione, Italy, in 2007. Bauer finished third with Trembath fourth.

Four-Letter 'L' Words Stories

This is a work of fiction, in that the author does not know of it having happened. But it could have.

Four-Letter 'L' Words

SHE pushed his arm away, giving something between a grunt and a sigh, muffled by the pillow. He thought she was awake but wasn't sure.

Her breathing deepened slightly, she inhaled and gave a deep sigh. She thought it would work.

It didn't.

Robert tried again, rolling towards her back so that the length of his upper body touched hers, sliding the inside of his forearm along her thigh until his arm encircled her trim waist.

'Go away,' she mumbled, pulling the hem of her nightie over her knees, 'I'm tired.'

'Annie ...' It was almost a plea, but this time he put his hand on her shoulder and tried to snuggle in close to her back.

'Go away,' she repeated, this time leaving no doubt she was awake. 'I'm tired, I'm not in the mood and I want to go to sleep.'

Robert's ardor was rapidly giving way to irritation.

'You're never in the mood lately.' His voice was calmer than he felt. His frustration was still clinging to hope.

'Talk to me, Annie ...'

'I don't want to talk, I'm tired, I want to go to sleep.'

'Well at least turn over and face me, you never even face me lately.'

'I can't sleep on my right side.'

Robert threw back the blankets and marched around the foot of the bed to the other side.

'Get over ...' he snapped. 'Get over that side and you'll be able to face the middle of the bloody bed.'

'I don't want to.'

'Well fuck you!'

Robert slammed the door behind him.

He awoke in the bed in the guest room and momentarily wondered where he was. It was still dark.

*

Annette lay there for a long time, thinking. She knew that by the time she woke, Robert would be gone to work. He kept his clothes for the next day in the spare room so as not to wake her and made his own breakfast. She felt guilty, but she couldn't help the way she felt about him, or about Josh.

Ah, Josh, the excitement machine. He was handsome, charming, educated and he made her laugh! Oh, and he was wealthy! Not that that was important, but she remembered her grandfather used to say: 'I've been rich and I've been poor and rich is better.'

Josh – the answer to a maiden's prayer. An old cliché, she thought, but pretty apt. So he was a few years younger. So what? Who cared? Certainly not her!

Annette lay staring into the dark, reflecting. What had she got herself into? How had it happened and how had it come to this? Josh wanted her to leave, but how could she? Robert was a decent man and God, how would their friends react, and their parents?

Her Mum and Dad loved Robert – their only disappointment had been that they hadn't had children.

Maybe that had something to do with it. They'd both wanted kids and Robert had come home devastated with the news that the doctor had told him his sperm count was such that it was 'unlikely' he'd ever become a father.

Annette had lied to him at the time, simply to ease the pain.

'Honey don't worry about it, please!' she'd begged him.

And then the lie.

'I had some tests done myself and they don't think I can have children either. I didn't tell you because I thought it would worry you and maybe there'd be a miracle.

'Anyway, I thought we'd have to try harder,' she had added with an impish grin, and they'd gone to bed and started the 'trying' campaign straight away.

Annette had loved him so much and he didn't deserve to have to carry the burden alone, she'd decided. If he was sterile, it wasn't going to happen. So what? It wasn't going to make any difference either. He hadn't chosen to be sterile, and she cared too much for him to have it matter. Better he retain his pride and think maybe it wasn't him.

Sure, she would have liked to have had Robert's children but it wasn't that big a deal. She wasn't particularly maternal and if it wasn't going to happen, it wasn't going to happen. What could possibly be served by telling him she'd twice been pregnant before she met him?

No-one else knew except that doctor at the clinic and he was hardly likely to broadcast what he'd been doing. No, no-one would ever know!

*

Sherry wrapped the second lot of sandwiches in cling-foil and took two bananas from the fruit bowl and two paper bags from the cupboard.

'Come on you kids, clean your teeth and Joey, pick up all that stuff in the lounge and put it in your bedroom. Are you ready Kylie? Give him a hand.'

Sherry was still in her tracksuit and sneakers. She'd walk the kids to school, tidy the house, have a quick shower and catch the tram in time to be at work by eleven. The 'lunch-time shift' they called it.

'Now you be a good boy today,' she told Joey at the schoolyard gate, 'and no fighting!'

Her girlfriend, who minded them after school, had an eight-year-old who was inclined to act 'the big kid' when his mother wasn't looking. He knew he could get Joey in because Joey was a terrier and had learned to stick up for himself from an early age. You had to in the flats, at least if you wanted to survive.

Kylie had them bluffed and they wouldn't fight when she was there. But Kylie was more likely to be in Rhiannon's room, talking about boys or listening to CDs.

'Mummy'll pick you up about half past six and if you've been good, we'll go to McDonalds for tea.'

The McDonalds promise was Sherry's 'secret weapon' — she knew it would work with the kids and it would get her out of having to cook tea when she got home. She would cook most nights and made sure they ate properly, or as properly as they could on a tight budget, but they deserved a treat occasionally and McDonalds kept them happy without costing too much.

She kissed Joey goodbye and noticed at the school grounds these days he would turn his cheek if there were other kids in the vicinity, and there always were. It was different at home, but no-one there was going to call him a sissy or a mummy's boy.

Kylie was a different matter. She wrapped her arms round Sherry's neck as she kissed her, then held the hug for a moment.

'I love you Mummy,' she said.

'I love you too Sweetheart,' said Sherry and watched her run off across the yard.

Sherry walked home reflecting on her little girl growing up. Twelve next year, only three years younger than she had been when she started in the business, working on the streets. Life had been different for her, though, and she felt she hadn't had much choice. Still, she was damned if she was going to let her daughter follow in her footsteps.

She hurried up the seven flights of stairs at the flats, silently cursing the lift mechanic, and went about the rest of her morning routine.

An hour and a half later she got off the tram and walked the block to Canterbury Tales. The girls used to laugh that it should have been called Canterbury Tails, but someone had said Mr. Chaucer wouldn't have liked that, whoever Mister bloody Chaucer was. Anyway 'Tales' had a bit more class, even Sherry knew that, and Canterbury Tales was a classy place.

*

Robert sat at his desk, looking at the figures but saw nothing.

Annie had been this way for ages now and it wasn't getting any better. In fact, if anything, it was getting worse. She wouldn't talk to him and Robert had got to the stage where he knew if there was an alternative, he would take it.

One of the secretaries had 'come on' to him at the Christmas party, but that was before the trouble with Annie had started and she was drunk anyway. In any case, he told himself, getting involved with someone you worked with, even for a fling, was asking for trouble.

The real problem was to find a way of patching up things with Annie, but quite apart from that, Robert was physically frustrated. He remembered his mate Jacko's favorite saying: 'It's got to be fed and it's too high above the ground to eat grass ...' Jacko was right, and it was becoming a major problem. He had even thought, fleetingly, about masturbation, but that was repugnant to him – worse than celibacy – and that option was quickly dismissed.

Robert recalled occasionally when the traffic was banked up in

Sanders Road, he had bypassed it by going 'the back way', through the side-streets for a kilometre or two. He'd noticed a place called 'Canterbury Tales'. It looked like an opulent old home with a classic old streetlight outside the front door. One night during the winter, when it was dark, he'd noticed the light was red.

Robert didn't get much work done, his mind racing, adrenalin pumping with apprehension as he pictured the scene in his mind's eye. But he knew what he was going to do.

*

Annette walked confidently across the foyer of the Plaza Hotel to the far end bank of lifts, the ones which serviced the upper floors. She pressed 22 and checked her hair and make-up in the mirror as the elevator glided swiftly past the lower floors. She looked elegant and she knew it. Her lipstick-pink tailored suit, black high-heels and matching bag complemented the glossy sheen of her black hair. She was starting to get what she liked to call 'smile lines' at the corners or her eyes, but so far she was probably the only one who had noticed them.

The elevator doors opened and Annette turned, as of habit, to the right and walked to the end of the corridor to number 222. The two suites on the 22nd floor had a panoramic view of the bay, framed by the mountains of the peninsular fading away in a semi-circle to the left and the forest of masts of the boats in the yacht club marina to the right.

The view reminded her of a line she had heard somewhere – on a clear day, you could see forever.

She knocked softly and a moment later Josh opened the door. They embraced and held each other for a long time. He kissed her, lingering for a moment, and stepped back to look at her.

'Champagne ...?' he asked.

'Of course,' she replied.

Josh poured the bubbles and raised his glass to his favorite toast.

'To four-letter L-words,' he said.

Annette knew it now – Life, Love, Lust and Luck, though not necessarily in that order.

'To four-letter L words,' she repeated.

They drank, then stood. Silent. His arm around her waist, they gazed out across the bay sparkling in the midday sun.

Josh put down his glass and began to undo the top button of her suit.

It was four o'clock when she left. She knew she'd be home by five, giving her adequate time to look like a housewife by the time Robert got home about 6.30.

She kissed Josh lightly, so as not to disturb her make-up and opened the door.

'Love you,' she said as she backed away.

'Love you too,' he replied.

'See you at tennis,' she smiled and headed down the corridor to the lifts.

*

Sherry sat in the plush lounge behind the beaded curtain, talking politics with Maree and Courtney. Business had been a bit slow since the usual lunchtime flurry and Vanessa, the new girl, was the only one who'd really been busy.

The conversation meandered from the bargains you could get at the market down the road on a Sunday morning, to how many of the stalls were run by Vietnamese. Then to the Government's immigration policies.

Sherry and Maree both had their views but they knew by now they were never going to win any sort of political argument with Courtney, who was working her way through university where she was majoring in politics.

'Let's hope she never wants to stand for Parliament,' Sherry had thought on more than one occasion. Politicians' pasts had a habit of coming back to bite them, Sherry thought, and a couple of years working at Canterbury Tales was hardly something Australia's first woman Prime Minister would want on her CV.

Anyway, Courtney seemed happy enough doing what she was doing and Sherry secretly admired the fact that she was trying to make a life for herself.

The chime sounded. Belle, at the reception desk, had a customer (or 'client' as she liked to call them) and it was time for one of them, at least, to go to work. Discussion over. But it didn't really matter because Courtney was 'blinding them with science' anyway.

One by one they swished through the curtain, which had hidden them from view, and did their little parade. When she first came to work here, Sherry had felt this part was like a meat market but she'd become used to it and it no longer worried her. After all, if you were going to be sensitive about something like that, you were in the wrong line of business, she'd decided.

Each in turn they introduced themselves by name, smiling seductively, then headed back behind the curtain. Actually, if the truth be known, if you absolutely didn't fancy the guy, the smile might be closer to a sullen glare but Belle didn't like that and if you wanted to keep your job, you didn't do it too often.

This time Sherry didn't even get to go back behind the curtain. The guy simply nodded to Belle and she said: 'He's all yours Sherry.'

He was a businessman type, not too bad at all, but he looked bloody terrified. She smiled, a genuine, warm smile, took him by the arm and led him down the hallway.

Sherry ushered Robert into what reminded him of a top class motel room, spacious, well-appointed and immaculate. The room was dominated by an oversized bed with satin sheets, liberally strewn with pillows. There were mirrors on the ceiling and in one corner was a shower and next to it a medium-sized spa, which he guessed would comfortably accommodate at least three or four people.

'What's your name, honey?' Sherry asked.

For a moment it seemed Robert needed an easier question, but he managed to overcome the mental block and stammered: 'Er, ah, Robert ...'

'Well it's nice to meet you Robert. Now if you'd like to get undressed and take a shower, I'll get the spa going, then I can give you a nice massage.'

Actually Sherry didn't mind the prospect of fucking Robert but, as of habit, she went into her routine of wasting as much time as possible on the preliminaries. Thirty minutes could be a long time to have to put in with some of the creeps whose money got them through the door.

As it turned out, though, she needn't have bothered.

'Er, don't worry about that,' said Robert, 'can we just, er, talk …?'

'Sure honey, just come and sit over here,' Sherry replied, sitting on the edge of the bed and patting the spot next to her.

It wasn't unusual for new clients to be a bit uptight and Sherry was well-practised in the art of putting them at ease. After all, she had to make them want to come back and they sure as hell weren't going to if they thought they hadn't got their money's worth.

Robert sat, uneasily, beside Sherry, who continued to lead the conversation in a bid to get him to relax.

'That's okay,' she said, 'but it's warm in here, so you're not going to need that jacket anyway.'

Robert was aware of beads of perspiration running down his back, although not necessarily from the warmth of the room.

Removing the jacket wasn't a bad idea, he told himself, so he allowed Sherry to assist him.

She took it and hung it on a coat-hanger, as if to allow him time to recompose himself, then returned to her spot beside him.

'We can probably do without the tie as well,' she said, and reached to undo it.

'No,' Robert protested, momentarily grabbing her wrist and pushing it away, 'I really mean it, I just want to talk.'

Even that didn't come as any great surprise to Sherry – it really wasn't that unusual. Men would want to tell her about their troubles – business, kids or, more commonly, wives who didn't understand them – and once she'd done her best to get them to relax and had established that they really didn't want to bonk her, she was only too happy to lend a sympathetic ear.

Sherry listened to Robert's story. She thought his wife was probably having an affair but he didn't ask for an opinion, so she kept it to herself. She gave him an extra few minutes and when it was time for him to go, she thought he'd probably be back.

'Come and see me again, any time,' she said and gave him a hug.

She wasn't thinking about the money and she didn't really mind if he wanted sex or not. She hoped he'd come back because she liked him. He had problems but he was a nice guy.

*

'Hi,' said Robert as he entered. He headed straight for the toilet, hoping that the greeting had come out sounding calmer than he felt.

Annette had heard the car drive in and had busied herself at the kitchen bench. She had changed into jeans and a loose fitting windcheater top and had her hair tied back in a short pony-tail. The black lace underwear was back in the drawer, ready to be washed tomorrow, and had been replaced by a set which probably should have found its way into the rag-bag some time ago.

'How was your day?' she asked when Robert emerged.

She didn't turn around and Robert, unusually, made no attempt to kiss her, or even give her a hug. He had no reason to think she would smell a whiff of another woman's perfume on him, but remembered Sherry had given him a hug as he was leaving. He wondered if he'd overdone the after-shave he'd surreptitiously slapped on when he washed his hands after going to the toilet.

'Yeah, okay,' he replied. 'What have you been up to?'

Annette could have done without that particular phrasing but there was no accusation in the tone and she was confident it was only a figure of speech.

'Not a lot,' she said. 'It's been a lovely day.'

It sounded as if she was talking about the weather, but she realized from the sudden bubble of warmth inside her that she wasn't. Still, that's the way it sounded to Robert, as it was supposed to.

'Yeah,' he replied in agreement, pulling the newspaper from his briefcase, turning on the television and heading for the bar in the corner of the lounge-room.

'Do you want a drink?' he asked, discovering his hands were trembling as the Scotch splashed into the glass.

'No, not at the moment.'

Annette would have killed for a drink but it was unusual for Robert to have one before dinner and she hardly ever did. Sometimes they had a bottle of wine with their meal, but that hadn't happened much lately. 'Anyway, I've probably had enough for one day,' she thought.

The football had started on TV and Robert planted himself firmly in front of it, watching intently without noticing who was playing. He'd never been an ardent follower of the game but took a passing interest when the Tigers were doing well. He probably averaged going to one game a season, but only when invited to go with a mate or as part of a group. He'd sometimes watch the Tigers if their game was on television, but most weeks he wouldn't know who they were playing.

'It's ready,' Annette called from the kitchen, carrying their meals to the table.

'Could I have mine here?' Robert replied, moving the newspaper and clearing a space on the coffee table in front of him.

Annette glanced at the screen as she handed him his plate and cutlery. She noticed the Swans were leading the Hawks by a goal. She was grateful Robert's sudden interest in the football eliminated the need for awkward small talk. If she got things done, she thought, she could be in bed before he finished watching.

*

Robert stopped for petrol on the way to work the following morning. He always paid by credit card. He kept the card in his wallet, which generally stayed in the console.

The wallet was there but the card wasn't. He thought nothing of it. It was not unusual for him to leave it in a pocket after using it.

He paid cash and headed for the freeway, trying to remember what he'd done with the card.

His memory-bank flicked through the possibilities.

'I probably left it on the bedside table.' He'd done that before.

'If it was there, how come I didn't pick it up with the cash?' That didn't make sense.

'When the hell was the last time I used it?'

'I didn't buy anything on the way home last night.'

'*Oh my God ...!*'

He nearly ran off the road.

*

Robert sat at his desk, deep in thought. The computer was on, but he didn't see any of the figures. How he could have been so stupid?

He knew he'd been pretty uptight about the whole business at Canterbury Tales, but uptight was one thing — lunacy was another!

He knew there was nothing immediate he could do and there was no point in rushing home to retrieve the card. He knew it would be in the pocket of the suit he wore yesterday and to go home would achieve nothing and would only raise suspicion.

There was no point even in contacting the brothel. He knew only too well all credit card transactions these days were electronic and the payment would already be on his statement, waiting to be mailed at the end of the month.

It hadn't even entered his head that you could actually pay by credit card at a brothel! Who the hell would be stupid enough to do that? He already knew the answer.

It must be bloody common, he thought. There was no question about it – the woman had simply taken his card, run it through the machine and got him to sign and he'd put it back in his pocket. It had all be so automatic. Like buying the petrol! Automatic pilot!

Robert couldn't concentrate. Certainly not on work and hardly on the problem at hand, but gradually he formulated in his mind what he had to do.

*

He phoned the local mail centre and was told the postman left at the same time every day and usually got to Bennett Street 'around 11'.

He rang the credit card company and established that statements were posted on the first of each month. Or the following Monday if the first happened to be at the weekend.

At least that gave him a time frame, he reflected.

*

It was 10 days until the end of the month. For Robert it seemed like 10 years. As the days dragged by, he found himself thinking about Oscar Wilde. He'd learned lots of quotations from Oscar's poetry at school. Suddenly one of them had taken up residence in his brain:

> 'All that we know who lie in gaol.
> Is that the wall is strong;
> And that each day is like a year,
> A year whose days are long ...'

Robert wasn't exactly in jail, but he was sure he knew how Oscar had felt. It was of little comfort. He was distracted and unable to eat, so much so that Annette began to notice, despite his efforts to be as natural as possible when she was around.

He was no longer sure what 'natural' or 'normal' were. Annie was still distant and the way he felt only made matters worse. Despite his efforts, they were becoming like strangers living under the same roof.

He constantly mentally berated himself for his own stupidity and convinced himself that the gods were deliberately torturing him by allowing this to happen in a 'long' month, of 31 days. But there was a redeeming feature, he told himself. At least the first of next month fell on a Friday, which meant the statement would arrive on the Monday. Almost certainly.

To Annette the change in Robert's attitude came as no surprise and she assumed it was her own fault. She still loved Robert – he was a good man and he'd done no wrong, but she simply couldn't feel the way about him she had before she met Josh.

*

It wasn't as if she'd set out to have an affair, Annette reminded herself – Josh had had simply been 'delivered' into her life.

Nicole had picked her up for tennis practice and hadn't been able to shut up. She'd started as soon as they got in the car.

'Well, dear, you've missed out badly,' she declared.

'Rachael brought her cousin last week and *he is a hunk*. Not only that, but he can play tennis, too. The girls are just about queuing up already but they needn't bother because he's mine, so eyes off! He's single and he must be rich. He drives a black Porsche. He's been in the London office of whoever-it-is for three years and he's just moved back here. Would you believe they've put him up at The Plaza until he finds himself somewhere to live? He comes from interstate originally, dunno where. Anyway he's going to need someone to show him around and that's going to be me!'

'Nic, you're babbling ...' Annette ventured.

She smiled at her sister's enthusiasm.

'It's all right for you single young things,' Annette said, 'but you seem to forget I'm an old married lady, so I don't qualify.'

How wrong she'd been.

Josh was everything Nicole had said he was and it was true, there was a queue.

Annette had been introduced and had partnered him for a couple of sets of mixed doubles, having been chosen to do so by Scott, the club pro, who had matched them up on ability rather than for any more devious reason. Scott was there purely for the tennis, which made him almost unique at the club.

Not only could Josh play, but he was the perfect gentleman, putting Annette at ease whenever she made an error and encouraging her every time she played a good shot.

She had mentally resolved to do whatever she could to help her sister's aspirations but, by the time the three of them, plus Rachael, had spent half an hour having a drink together in the clubrooms after training, Annette was only too aware it was not her sister Josh was interested in.

Josh had the luxury of mostly being able to work whatever hours suited him. He usually made it to practice, especially the evening sessions, and quickly earned a spot in the men's A-grade squad. With the men he was a fierce competitor. He worked on his game and his fitness and it showed.

He was charming to everyone but showed not the slightest interest in any of the gaggle of women who threw themselves at him. After a few weeks the whisper in the ladies' locker room was that he must be gay.

Annette knew he wasn't.

*

As the end of the month drew closer, Robert became more and more 'toey', but, try as he might, there was nothing he could do about it.

In his moments of clarity he realized the irony of the situation. In his desperation to prevent Annie finding out about his visit to the brothel he was worsening the relationship he was trying to save. The quality of their communication had dropped even further and, despite his wife not going out of her way to improve it, Robert accepted in his own mind that the fault was mainly his.

Annette had noticed but assumed it was her coolness toward her husband, which she couldn't help, and the vibes he was getting which had changed his normally relaxed demeanor to something she didn't recognize.

It came as a slight relief that the 1st fell on a Friday and Robert had decided to spend the weekend feigning symptoms of an illness which by Monday would preclude him from going to work. Then he received the intra-office memo on the notepaper headed *'From the desk of the Managing Director'*:

> **'Your attendance is required at breakfast in the boardroom next Monday to meet the Chairman of Directors of the New York office of LOMAX INTERNATIONAL, Mr. Harrison Dillard. 7.30 am SHARP.'**

'*Oh fuck …*' thought Robert. '*Fuck, fuck, fucking fuck …*'

The way he felt, he wasn't going to have to *feign* illness after all. But he *was* going to have to be at the breakfast.

*

Annette didn't notice Robert had left earlier than usual on Monday morning. All she knew was that, as usual, he wasn't there when she got up. The day looked pretty much the way her Mondays usually did – put on the washing, vacuum the house, then tennis with the girls at 11. Josh wouldn't be there, but she'd see him at practice on Wednesday evening. Then she'd see him on Thursday night when, so far as Robert knew, she had to attend the meeting of the sub-committee to which she'd been recently elected.

She smiled to herself. It really was a sub-committee, except there were only two of them and it wasn't often they talked about tennis.

Thursday nights were regular, the occasional daytime trysts a bonus.

She had just finished vacuuming when her mobile phone rang.

It struck her as unusual. When any of the girls rang, or Robert, they'd ring on the landline.

'Hello, this is Annette …'

'Hello Darling, can you talk?'

Her heart skipped a beat.

'I can indeed, and how are you?'

'I'm fine, you?'

She was suddenly apprehensive. Josh had never rung her before. The only times they'd spoken on the phone were on a couple of occasions when she'd called him at the hotel. They'd discussed the matter and decided it was just too risky. Unless, of course, it was an emergency.

'Is anything wrong?' she asked.

'No, not at all. It's just I'm not far away and I thought if you were home I could pick up those entry forms for the tournament; they've got to be in by Friday.'

Annette's mind raced. It was safe enough, she thought. Robert was at work and, in any case, Josh was a member of the tennis club.

She wasn't expecting anyone to drop by and, even if they did, she had a valid reason for him being there. She'd planned to post him the forms on her way to tennis and they were on the kitchen bench waiting.

'That'd be lovely. How soon?'

'As long as it takes to get off the freeway and find my way to your place.'

'See you soon.'

Annette went into overdrive. She tidied, brushed her hair and quickly put on some make-up. She looked pretty swishy in a track-suit, she knew that, so that wasn't a problem. After all, he'd hardly expect her to be doing the housework in a ball-gown, would he? She had just turned on the electric jug when the door-bell rang. On the radio, the announcer began the 10 o'clock news.

She hadn't expected it to be the way it was. They almost devoured each other.

Annette had a momentary mental battle. Common sense versus lust.

She disengaged herself from Josh's embrace and took him by the hand.

'Come with me,' she said.

The news-reader in the kitchen started the weather report and the jug boiled and switched itself off. They didn't notice.

*

Robert wasn't sure why but he helped himself to a plate of food from the buffet. He couldn't eat and simply poked at it. At least that way he didn't look conspicuous, he thought. Not as conspicuous as if he threw up, which was the other option.

He managed a cup of hot, black coffee and tried to listen to Harrison Dillard.

For Christ's sake, the big brass *never* visited them. Why today, of all days?

Robert found himself looking at his watch every five minutes.

He didn't realise his agitation was showing until Dave, sitting next to him, took the opportunity to lean over during a round of applause.

'You all right, mate?' he asked.

'I just don't feel too good,' Robert replied honestly.

He knew the mail usually arrived at about 11, but he wanted to be home by 10.30, in case it was early. He also knew it took him four minutes from his desk to the car park – he'd timed it – and that, on average, the drive home took about 55 minutes. He had to allow an hour, total.

The big boss droned on, about financial projections, new projects, market image – all the usual claptrap. Robert probably looked like he was listening but he hadn't heard a thing. He dared not leave, but as the time ticked past nine o'clock he started to think about it.

Dillard sat down. The chairman was thanking him.

'Now we've finished with the formalities I'd be grateful if you'd stay for an informal chat for a few minutes,' he was saying, 'Mr Dillard would like to meet some of you.'

The 'invited guests' left their tables and assembled in groups, 'like bloody sheep,' thought Robert, as the waitresses served coffee. Robert was about to make his apologies and bolt when he realized the chairman and Dillard were heading for his group.

'Jesus!' he thought and glanced furtively at his watch. It was 9.22.

Eleven minutes later he was in the car. If there'd been a record from the boardroom to his desk to the car park, he'd broken it. And that was even allowing for the 30 seconds he had taken to tell his secretary that he 'felt terrible' was going home and that he'd ring her later. He knew that at least the first two statements were the truth.

The traffic on the freeway wasn't too bad but as he got to the off-ramp he was stuck behind a car being driven by a man in a hat and a woman driving a Land Cruiser, both of whom obviously had nowhere to go and all day to get there.

Robert wasn't normally an impatient person, but today was different. He knew it would take another 10 minutes from when he left the freeway. It was 10.15.

Josh could feel himself becoming agitated. He hadn't intended this to happen. The passionate, animal desire had taken over, but now it was finished he found he couldn't relax. Annette, snuggled beside him, was lost in the warmth of contentment. Josh glanced at the digital clock on the bedside table. It was 10.15.

*

Annette sensed Josh's unease.

'It's okay,' she reassured him. 'Robert's at work and there won't be any visitors. Just relax for a few minutes.'

'I'd really better get going,' Josh replied.

'I only came to say hello and get the entry-forms,' he added with a grin.

'Do you want to have a shower?' Annette asked.

Suddenly Josh discovered all he wanted to do was to leave as quickly, albeit gracefully, as he could.

'I won't, Darl,' he replied. He did his best to sound cool and composed. 'I've got to go back to the hotel, so I'll have one there.'

Annette hooked her leg around him and held him tight. Josh hesitated. Her hand began to slide downwards. She felt him tense.

'Darling I have to go,' Josh said. He kissed her quickly and extricated himself.

Annette took the hint and headed to the ensuite, returning with a warm, damp face-cloth.

Josh wiped the wet bits and dressed quickly as Annette pulled her tracksuit back on and straightened her hair.

'Don't want the neighbors to think I've just got out of bed, do I?" she grinned mischievously.

Robert cursed as the pedestrian lights at the shopping centre turned red. The dashboard clock told him it was 10.23.

By the time they walked to the car, Josh looked every inch the well-dressed, handsome young executive who had entered the house a short time earlier. Not that anyone was watching, or timing them, but had they done so they would have noted the visit had taken 22 minutes and concluded at 10.23.

Annette stood on the footpath and waited as Josh got into his car. She waved, almost formally, as he drove off then turned and noticed the postman approaching on his motorbike. She gave him a smile and a 'thank you' as he stopped and handed her a small sheaf of letters.

She sorted through them as she walked back to the house and noted that all but one had 'windows' – probably bills, she thought. She picked up the knife she kept beside the fruit-bowl on the kitchen bench and, one by one, slit the envelopes.

She opened the first of them and had started to read when she heard the remote controlled garage door and a car in the driveway.

Robert had not noticed the one oncoming car, a black Porsche, as he entered Bennett Street. He wasn't sure he'd ever actually seen his local postman and didn't even know what mode of transport he used to deliver the mail, but he was looking.

He was more than halfway along the long, tree-lined street when he saw the yellow-clad figure on a motorbike riding along the footpath. He was coming toward him, which meant he'd already been past No 42!

Robert went cold, but by the time he drove into the garage less than a minute later, his palms were sweating, beads of perspiration were beginning to break out on his forehead and in his armpits and his breathing had become shallow. But he didn't notice.

The thought flashed through his head: *'It could only have been a minute.'* He half held his breath, turned off the ignition and headed for the letterbox.

It was empty.

Annette's first impulse was to freeze in panic, but it lasted only a moment. She deftly replaced the letter in its envelope, dropped it with the others and dashed to the bedroom. She pulled up the covers, straightened the pillows, threw on the bedspread and dived for the walk-in wardrobe which doubled as a dressing-room.

She had most of her tennis clothes on by the time the back door opened. She pretended not to hear it. She finished dressing but could feel her heart pounding as she headed towards the kitchen.

Robert was standing near the sink with a glass of water in his hand. Had Annette been more composed, she may well have noticed he was clutching it tightly and that the water wouldn't stay steady.

'Oh, hello,' she said, as casually as she could manage.

'I thought I heard something. What are you doing home?'

Had Robert been more composed, he may have noticed the slight quaver in her voice. But he didn't.

'I'm not well,' he replied. 'I came home.'

Robert had already seen the letters on the bench and had noticed the envelopes had been opened. He averted his eyes from her gaze. He didn't look directly at the letters but they were all he was aware of in his peripheral vision. He knew the contents of the top one were protruding slightly but it was face down and he couldn't tell if there was a logo on the envelope.

He waited for something to happen.

'*Shit,*' thought Annette, '*he's going to go to bed.*'

But Robert was Robert and he was hardly likely to notice, was he? He wasn't usually even aware of her perfume unless she put it on with a ladle – how likely could he be to notice anyone else's smell in the bed?

'Oh, Christ,' she thought. '*What if there's a wet patch?*'

She knew there was nothing she could do about it. She would come up with some sort of feasible reason later, if she had to.

Annette realized she didn't want Robert to find out, but she wasn't sure why. The panic and the urgency hit her like a pile-driver. Instantly, she knew what she had to do but didn't know how to do it.

She needed time to think, but now was not the time. For now, she had to survive. She battled to stay calm.

'Can I get you anything?' she asked.

For Robert, the scene was starting to unfold in slow motion.

Had he been able to identify his emotions he probably would have recognized both puzzlement, then a minute, seeping start of relief.

He could think only that the eruption for which he'd been bracing himself didn't seem to be happening. '*She couldn't possibly be taking it this well if she knew,*' he thought. '*Could she?*'

'I'll be okay,' he ventured. He was aware of his voice, but it seemed surreal.

'There's aspirin and stuff in the bathroom cupboard,' she continued, 'and there's some soup in the fridge. You can heat it up in the microwave – it might make you feel better.'

Robert was vaguely aware of his tension beginning to ease imperceptibly but he still seemed to be observing from outside his body, as if watching two actors in a play.

Annette was still talking.

'I'll have to go or I'll be late for tennis,' she continued.

He couldn't pick her tone.

'I'll see you later,' she said.

She turned to go.

'I'll take this one ...'

She picked up the top letter and walked out the door.

Robert stood motionless as Annette's car backed down the driveway and drove off along Bennett Street. Suddenly he thought he was going to be ill and dashed for the bedroom and the toilet in the ensuite.

Annette's mobile phone rang.

'Hello Darling,' said the voice, 'are you having a nice day?'

She tingled at the sound of his voice. Her resolve evaporated.

'I sure am,' she replied. 'I had a handsome gentleman caller and I just got a letter from my brother in England. So how's your day been?'

'Mine's been great,' Josh said, 'but I'll have to get you to do me a favor. This wicked young lady had her way with me and I'm pretty sure I've left my watch on her bedside table ...'

A Breeder's Lament
Stories

During his time as a journalist, the author was simultaneously editor of both the monthly magazine Australian Reinsman and what was then Victorian Trotting Weekly, later to become Australian Harness Racing Weekly. He also bred, trained and drove harness horses with considerable success. This true story was published in 1982 and won the Australian Harness Racing Council's coveted 'Joseph Coulter Award' for the best story of the year in all categories.

A Breeder's Lament
Or, Why Trembath Isn't Roman Coffee

DO you remember when the Pope John Paul I died ...? Well I do, and I'm not even a Roman Catholic.

It was September 29, 1978 and I have a very good reason for remembering. It meant I had to make the coffee for the staff at Trotting Weekly for a week.

Perhaps the significance of all that might not be immediately apparent, so maybe I'd better explain.

Back in those days Trotting Weekly, Australian Reinsman's sister publication, had a staff of four – one Protestant, me, and three Roman Catholics.

That was really of no consequence at all and the matter of religion was seldom mentioned, but it was the basis for a chance remark one day, the significance of which will become apparent.

We used to virtually live on coffee in the office but because I was male and busy (some would say chauvinistic), not to mention being 'the boss', I seldom took a turn at making it, the task usually falling to the lot of one of the two girls.

This particular day Jill Pasco, who at the time was assistant editor of Trotting Weekly, apparently was a trifle grumpy about something or other and seemed intent on stirring up trouble. Rallying the others to her cause, she demanded to know 'How come it's us Catholics that make the coffee all the time? When are you going to make it?'

'Leave me alone,' I replied. 'When the Pope dies I'll make it every day for a week.'

I hadn't given much thought to the Pope's health at the time and for all I knew he might have lasted another 50 years. In any case, it shut them up temporarily and Jill went and got the coffee.

Pope Paul VI died about a month later.

The rest of the staff didn't know whether to laugh or cry. They all went into suitable mourning for His Holiness, of course, while simultaneously having the time of their lives demanding cups of coffee about every five minutes for the next week. It's a wonder they didn't all die of caffeine poisoning.

The week passed, slowly, and at its conclusion the old familiar demand was made once more: 'So when are you going to make the coffee again?'

The answer was obvious. 'Same conditions,' I replied.

'I'll make it for a week when the Pope dies.' I even permitted myself a smug grin. I'd seen pictures of the newly elected Pope John Paul I and he looked in the prime of life.

The historians will tell you that the shortest reign in the history of the Roman Catholic Church was that of Pope John Paul I.

It was early on the morning of September 29, 1978 that I was walking up to the back paddock at home, transistor radio in my pocket, to check on my broodmare Winning, who was due to foal.

The news headlines almost stopped me in my tracks ...

'Pope John Paul the first is dead ...'

I know it's going to sound sacrilegious, and it probably was, but I remember distinctly my first thought. 'My God,' it went through my mind, 'I've got to make the coffee for another week.'

At that instant I saw the foal.

The mare hadn't really been expected to foal for another day or two, and the baby colt frisking about beside her had taken me a little by surprise. Still, he was a bonny little fellow and obviously had had no trouble making his way into the world without any assistance from me.

Arriving at the office, this time it was me who didn't know whether to laugh or cry. I was delighted with the foal but the thought of having to put up with another week of persecution as a coffee-slave was almost too much. Nevertheless, sometimes you have to put up with these things, so I made the first cup of coffee, over which we discussed the events of the morning.

A couple of cups later, with a strong feeling of Catholic oppression beginning to take over, I determined to fight back, so when asked what I was going to call the foal I declared he was to be known as 'George Ringo'.

'If the Pope can call himself after half of The Beatles, then the foal can be called after the other half,' I explained.

The howls of protest could have been heard in Vatican City and this time, I suspected, they were serious.

After having various aspects of my pedigree explained to me, not to mention that there was every chance that The Divine Hand of Providence was about to zot me, I decided that rather than risk a Catholic uprising, I'd better revise my ideas.

So, appropriately, the colt became known to his friends as 'Coffee' and it was generally agreed, with no protests from the Catholics, that when I applied for a racing name for the youngster the first choice would be 'Roman Coffee'.

But that day never came.

With two yearlings and the usual number of bills that year, it was decided that one of them would have to be sold. One of the youngsters was by the fashionable sire Hilarious Way, while the other* was by the then relatively unknown sire Golden Kenny. The sizes of the bills decreed that it was going to have to be the one who would bring the higher price who would have to go, so Coffee was prepared for the yearling sales.

He was knocked down for $4,300 to Mildura trainer-reinsman Frank Cavallaro, on behalf of stable clients Tony and Don Sergi. I gave Coffee a pat, wished his new connections luck, and wondered if I'd ever see him again.

It was a few months later that John Peck, from the Australian Trotting Council, phoned me at the office.

'We've got a name application here from someone wanting to call a horse "Trembath",' he said. 'What do you want us to do?'

'What's the horse?' I asked, and was informed it was a yearling colt by Hilarious Way from Winning.

Coffee.

I told John I'd ring him back and immediately booked a call to Frank Cavallaro.

'What's going on?' I asked him. 'Are you trying to get even with me?'

But Frank assured me that that was anything but the case.

'Mate, he's not only the best young horse I've ever had, he's the best young horse I've ever seen,' he said. 'We thought we'd like to name him after you.'

With a story like that there's not much you can say, so I rang John Peck and gave him permission to pass the name. So Coffee became Trembath.

It's history now, of course, that Frank Cavallaro's judgment proved spot on and ultimately Trembath accumulated more than $68,000 in stakes – an imposing sum at the time – from more than 20 wins and numerous placings.

Only Garry's Advice and San Simeon had ever earned more stake-money by the Christmas of their three-year-old year in the history of harness racing in Australia.

Trembath, in fact, can be deemed most unlucky to have been born in the same year as such an outstanding colt at Garry's Advice, who as a juvenile broke every record in the book.

On two occasions Trembath ran Garry's Advice to a half head in finals of classics and on another occasion he finished third.

Trembath finished his two-year-old season with a little over $23,000 in stakes, but had Garry's Advice not been in those races the additional prize-money he would have earned would have taken him to within a whisker of the Australian two-year-old stakes record previously held by San Simeon, who was undefeated in the first 29 races of his career.

One person who recognised the youngster's potential was top Western Australian horseman Phil Coulson, who made the Sergi brothers an unsuccessful offer of $100,000 for him.

With figures like those floating about, it's only natural that people often ask if I'm sorry I sold him.

They can't seriously want an answer to a question like that but it's still a fact that any breeder who takes youngsters to yearling sales hopes they do well for their new owners. After all, there's always the chance that a satisfied customer will come back again.

In the case of Trembath, however, any further interest in his career on my part is purely academic. His mother, Winning, died prematurely, probably of snake-bite, at the age of 12, just about the time her son was really starting to hit the high-spots.

In trotting, as in life, one quickly learns to accept the decrees of Fate and undoubtedly there are some who will say I have been justly punished for my sacrilegious jibes at my Catholic workmates.

And perhaps they're right because it wasn't until much later that I realised how close I really went to taking Coffee home with me from the sales.

My original reserve price was $5,000 but the sale was poor and when I went to the auctioneer's box I dropped it to $4,250. There's no way

I would have taken any less, so it seems that had Tony Sergi not bid $4,300, I would have taken the youngster home.

Throughout most of the world, all horses are recognised as having their 'birthday' on August 1, but, as chance would have it, Sergi mentioned to me at the trots one night that Trembath had just had his real birthday, on August 29.

I told him he was wrong and that the colt had been born on September 29, but he was insistent and revealed that the only yearlings he'd even considered for purchase that year were those who were August foals.

I checked later in the sale catalogue and there it was ... 29/8/78 – August 29.

But the date in the catalogue was a misprint. I'd just never noticed.

Of all the foals I've ever bred, I think Coffee's birth date is the only one I'd be sure about. He was born on September 29. I remember it well.

> *Footnote: The yearling the author kept later raced as Dark Dreamer, the best horse he had during his career in harness racing. Dark Dreamer went on to win stakes of more than $102,000 from 19 wins, among them the Group 1 Tasmanian Easter Cup and Group 2 Tasmanian Easter Plate. Of the 13,500 foals bred in Australia in the 1978 season, Dark Dreamer's career stake-earnings ranked him No 2, behind Garry's Advice. Trembath, who grew up in the same paddock, ranked No 5.*

Catherine In Wonderland
Stories

Written in 2002, this story is 'creative non-fiction' or 'story truth', in that it is based on a series of incidents the author believes to be true.

Catherine In Wonderland

SHE lay on her back, knees bent, legs spread, the child-woman with bruises in the crease of her elbows and along her forearms.

Eyes closed, with her mind in Wonderland, looking for Alice.

Above her he heaved and panted and grunted, thrusting against her pelvis.

He had told her his name, as if to make it more personal, but she hadn't been listening, or couldn't remember. He was fifty bucks.

She needed the money for the drugs. She needed the job for the money and she needed the drugs to be able to get through the job.

Perhaps he'd said his name was Barry, but what did it matter? Just another faceless face. Just another prick, in both senses of the word. 'Ha, I made a funny!' she thought.

The grunting had stopped and he lay on her. Heavy. Heavy enough to make her move, to half-wriggle out from underneath. He flopped sideways and lay motionless beside her, one arm draped across her. She fought the urge to sleep.

She knew the rules. Who cared if you were 'out of it', or just plain exhausted, sleep was not an option. It had happened once and had nearly cost her her job.

'F'Chrissakes Cathy,' Belle had screamed at her, 'what do you think you're doing? You're not here to sleep with 'em ...'

They'd sent her home in a cab and docked her pay, then she'd had to put up with one of Belle's lectures. Belle wasn't too bad really and what she'd said made a lot of sense.

'Cathy honey, they're not going to ask for you next time if you go to sleep in the middle of it. Half of 'em still think they're Rudolph bloody Valentino y'know.'

That was all, but she knew that next time there wouldn't be a next time. There were plenty more junkies to take her place, or smug college girls 'working' their way through university.

'I'd rather have you, love,' Belle had confided to her once. 'Those other bitches think their shit doesn't stink ...' What Belle really meant, though, was that the junkies were easier to control.

At least this was better than it used to be, she thought. The waterbed was comfortable, the room was immaculate but most of all it was safe. Or at least as close as you were going to get to safe. Not like the old days, months ago, stepping off the kerb into a car beside someone who wasn't going to change your life, but might end it.

The money wasn't as good now she had to give half of it away and it took twice as long, twice as many faceless freaks, to get enough. And how much was ever going to be enough? She had gone from pot through the whole list, downhill or uphill, depending on which way you thought of it – speed, crack, coke, ecstasy, then 'the real stuff', horse, the big H.

It cost her a fortune to support her habit but it was more reliable these days, more ordered. The cycle just kept going round – the 'faceless faces', the money, the drugs ...

It had started four years ago, in another lifetime, when she was 12.

In those days she'd been Catherine, or at least she was to her grandpa, whom she adored. She remembered when she was a little girl, Grandpa sitting on the side of her bed reading her *Alice In Wonderland*.

'Where's Wonderland?' she'd asked him and Grandpa had told her it was just over the hill behind the big, white houses on Maple Road with their high fences and heavy, black wrought-iron gates and their shiny cars where they used to pass on the tram.

'Where does Alice live?' she'd ask him, standing on the seat as they went by, and occasionally Catherine would catch a glimpse of one of the elegantly-dressed ladies who lived in the houses and dream of the day she'd join them.

Catherine loved going with Grandpa past Wonderland and thought what good fun it would be to go with Alice to a tea-party.

Her mother had come home from the funeral drunk and abusive and there had been no more bedtime stories.

*

The other kids were smoking joints in the toilets or down in the far corner of the school ground, under the cypress trees where it was dry and the darkness of the shade provided a safe place to abandon safety.

Joining in hadn't seemed like any big deal at the time, it was just what everybody did. And anyway, the smoke made her feel good, grown-up, and it was easier to face going home to her drunken mother, who would belt the crap out of her, just for something to do.

Sometimes she'd get lucky and her mother would be passed out on the couch, or in the bedroom giggling and moaning with one of her pig boyfriends. Catherine hated them and the way they undressed her with their leering eyes and groped her when her mother wasn't looking.

The smoke made her feel euphoric and full of the joy of life. She'd mother her little sisters and bring in the washing if her mother had done it, or do it herself if she hadn't.

It was her thirteenth birthday, the day he had grabbed her and dragged her into the bedroom. She couldn't remember his name either, but she remembered his hideous, twitching prick and how he'd snatched a handful of her hair at the back of her head and pushed her face down onto it.

She remembered her clenched teeth, the pain as her head was jerked back and the whack of his butcher's hand across the side of her face.

'Open yer mouth ya little bitch ...' he yelled and she had been too scared not to.

He shuddered and spurted and filled her mouth and her throat and released his grip and she retched and ran from the room and threw up on the lounge-room floor before she made it to the door.

She'd glimpsed her mother lying naked on the bed and assumed she was unconscious but hadn't been quite sure. She was sure the next time, though, because the next time her mother had been sitting up.

From then on it was always going to be easy for the sleaze in the schoolyard to sell the little white pills to Catherine, and easier for her to want them than to get the money to pay.

She wasn't stupid — she knew how the other girls got money and at first it had been almost an adventure. She'd had money to spare and any was a lot when you'd been used to having none, but it was never going to last.

'Where did you get all this you little whore?' screamed her mother, bursting into the kitchen brandishing a fistful of notes as Catherine dropped her school-bag on the table.

'Don't you call me a whore,' yelled Catherine, 'and give me that ...'

She surprised herself. She'd never stood up to her mother before, even when the old bitch had ransacked the place looking for grog money and emptied the little kids' money-boxes.

But it made no difference – Catherine didn't see the money again but noticed the next day there were half a dozen bottles of cheap Scotch in the corner instead of the usual one or two. That night she packed her worldly goods in a bag and met Deb on the corner as usual.

'Hi Cathy,' came the greeting, 'what's with the bag – ya runnin' away from home?'

'Yep,' she'd replied, 'I'm comin' to live with you.'

Living with Deb was fine. They laughed a lot and she didn't miss school one bit. They'd sleep half the day and work half the night and spend most of the time spaced out on the stuff Deb got for both of them from the lunk she liked to refer to as her 'manager'. She missed her sisters and she missed her grandpa and she missed Wonderland, but mostly life was just a haze with soft edges and it didn't really seem to matter any more.

But Catherine knew that it did matter. Sure, she was Cathy now, but the Catherine her grandpa had loved still lived somewhere down inside and just occasionally, when the tram took her along Maple Road, it would all come back.

One day, she would live in one of the big white houses, she mused.

*

Somewhere in the background Billy Joel sang 'Piano Man'.

*'... I'm sure that I could be a movie star,
if I could get out of this place ...'*

It all seemed so long ago, she thought.

Barry had lumbered to his feet and started putting on his clothes.

From Insult To Injury Stories

Written in 2002, soon after the author won the gold medal in the Men's 300m hurdles at the World Masters' Games at Olympic Park in Melbourne, this is a true story.

From Insult To Injury

I KNOW writing about winning a gold medal at the World Masters' Championships sounds self-indulgent, but bear with me, it's not like that.

The fact is I've got no particular ambitions to show my medal to anyone other than my grandchildren. Except for one bloke!

Let me paint the scene: We're back a couple of months before the Games and this particular morning I'm jogging through the leafy back-blocks of Eltham to the local oval to do some training on the grass.

A few hundred metres from the oval there's a tip-truck parked beside the track with the truckie obviously having his breakfast/morning-tea/lunch or whatever you call it when you're eating a pie about 10am. At a guess I'd say he's about half my age (i.e. about 30) and twice my weight (i.e. about 160kg) although perhaps that's a tad uncharitable, but not much. In any case, he's in proper truckies' uniform – big bushy beard, blue singlet, tatts etc., and obviously doesn't have anything particularly urgent to attend to at the time.

Anyway, it's a pretty quiet spot, there's no-one else around and as I jog past I offer the usual Australian greeting: 'How are yer, mate ...?'

Nothing. Not even a nod.

Now perhaps he was deaf and couldn't lip read, but I don't think so.

What I do think is that sometimes, despite the silence, you just know there's a thought-conversation going on.

And in this case it went something like this:

Truckie: *Doddering old fool ...*

Me: *Get stuffed. Fat slob.*

Now even if he was a mind-reader, I was still going to be okay because he couldn't get his truck where I was going and I knew if it came to the worst, there was no way he could catch me on foot.

But I digress.

A short time later I arrived at the oval and was jogging quietly around the perimeter when, in the space of one stride, I was in mortal agony. Something had happened to my calf. I didn't know what but was pretty sure it was career-threatening, or possibly even life-threatening (as you do!). Ultimately it turned out to have been just a cramp, but that's not the point.

At the time I couldn't walk, let alone run, and I wasn't at all sure how I was going to get home, which was about a kilometre away.

As it was, after a bit of self-massage I set off, doing the best I could, knowing full well I had no choice. If I didn't, I would certainly die of exposure and my body wouldn't be found until the next time the local footy team played at home.

Ultimately, of course, as I limped painfully back the way I'd come, I rounded the bend to where, only a few minutes earlier, with long smooth strides, I'd swept past the truckie. He was still there.

This time I made no attempt at greeting, or even making eye contact. I didn't need to. He didn't say a word, but the mental telepathy began the instant I came into view.

HAH ..! TOLD YOU SO. SILLY OLD PRICK.

Yes, I'd like to show *him* my medal!

Only Mugs Try At Trials Stories

Written in 1991, this is a true story.

Only Mugs Try At Trials

The Diamond Valley Harness Racing Club was formed in the late 1970s and a track was built at Yarrambat Park, on the north-eastern outskirts of Melbourne.

While the land came at no cost, the club had to raise the finance for developing and maintaining the track once it was built. Various fundraising activities were undertaken but undoubtedly the most successful was the 'sweep' which was conducted on the main race at the trials at Yarrambat each Sunday morning.

Strictly speaking it probably was illegal, but nobody seemed too worried and patrons were admitted free but were asked to buy a two-dollar ticket in the sweep, which almost everyone was only too happy to do. Half the money went to the club and the other half was divided among the drawers of the first two horses in the designated trial, with 80 per cent going to the lucky patron who drew the winner and 20 per cent to the drawer of the second horse.

In any case, it was a bit of harmless fun, it didn't cost much and it seemed that if you kept buying tickets long enough you eventually would draw a horse and maybe even the winner.

In those days I was training and driving an old horse named Cele Bevel, who was far from being a dud, eventually finishing his career with five wins and innumerable minor placings to his credit. Anyway, Cele was one of those clever old horses who had worked out that trials were trials and races were races and that only mugs tried at the trials.

We had the business down to such a fine art, in fact, that in assessing how he was going at any particular time I concluded that if he finished within 40 metres of the place getters in a maiden class, even at the trials, he probably was going well enough to be a winning chance in his own class at the races.

Seeing that buying a ticket in the sweep was almost mandatory, there was nothing unusual about a driver in the sweep race having one of his opponents running for a few dollars which, on occasions, led to a little skulduggery.

After all, they were only trials. You didn't have to try, and if you happened to have the leader running for 50 or 60 dollars, you would have to have something wrong with you if you got up on your own horse and beat him.

Anyway, on this particular morning I was driving around behind the barrier when one of my opposing reinsmen, whom I shall identify only as 'Dougie' for fear of embarrassing him, came up and informed me that he had drawn my horse, Cele Bevel, in the sweep.

'Can you win?' Dougie asked. 'It's worth 52 dollars and I really need the money ...'

Knowing Dougie, I was well aware that he wasn't joking, but knowing Cele I was also aware that he had plenty of problems. In any case, it didn't matter to me and I was only too happy to help if I could, so I told Dougie what he had to do.

'The only hope you've got,' I said, 'is to go straight to the lead, let me drop in behind you, go flat out all the way, then wait for me at the finish ...'

Away we went from the mobile barrier, with Dougie driving his horse to the lead like a man possessed. I was able to wake Cele Bevel up enough to get him in on the rails behind Dougie and we began hurtling around the circuit as if it was at least the Inter Dominion Championship, if not the Inter-Galactic Pace.

Not surprisingly there weren't any challengers from the rear and we stormed around the home turn with Dougie in front and me right behind him. Straightening for the run home I eased Cele Bevel to the outside to challenge and immediately received the predictable response – 'you've got to be kidding' – transmitted down the reins.

Still, I was well aware of how important the money was to a battler like Dougie, so I got to work and gradually we began to draw alongside. Then, suddenly, Dougie was faced with a moment of truth.

It wasn't often that he drove a winner, even at the trials, and as I struggled to reach him, suddenly I became aware that Dougie was facing a major emotional crisis – whether to give his horse a whack on the rump and win the trial or whether to let me win, which was going to mean defeat, albeit with a profit of 52 dollars.

For one horrifying moment, Dougie's mind obviously left the body and he actually raised his whip. It was only when I yelled at him 'Dougie, what are you doing? For God's sake don't hit him!' that he returned to sensibility.

He took hold, Cele Bevel reluctantly poked his nose in front and went on to record what probably was the most memorable trials win of his career. Dougie collected his 52 dollars and I later received the only 'sling' I have ever got at the trials – Dougie bought me a hamburger at the breakfast caravan!

Rest Easy, Girl
Stories

Written in 1989 after the death of the author's first horse, this is a true story.

During his journalistic career, the author founded what originally was Victorian Trotting Weekly, later to become Australian Harness Racing Weekly, and was editor for more than 20 years. The following story was published in June, 1989 and won the Australian Harness Racing Council's 'Joseph Coulter Award' for the year's best story in all categories of its awards.

Rest Easy, Girl

ONE evening last week, an old mare named Moonlight Sky lay down for the last time and peacefully drifted off to horse heaven.

'So what?' you may ask, and with some justification, for nowhere is her name chipped in stone, nor is it to be found among the list of Australian harness racing's all-time greats.

Only if you can remember trotting as it was in Western Victoria in the early sixties, or if you are an ardent student of breeding would you be likely to have heard of her.

But if there had been no Moonlight Sky, I greatly doubt there ever would have been a 'Trotting Weekly', or certainly not one as we know it today.

I first met 'Helen', as I always knew her, at the Wright Stephensons' sales complex, over the road from Flemington racecourse, on July 1, 1963.

At that stage I had been working as a cadet journalist on the Wimmera Mail-Times at Horsham for about 18 months, spending most of my days off at the stables of the Wimmera's most prominent trainer, Jack McKay, at Minyip.

My 'landlord' and friend, Max Parish, who was the top driver around the Wimmera circuit at the time, worked for 'Minyip Jack' and gradually taught me the basics of the trotting business.

Learning to drive was a slower process because, initially anyway, the lessons had to be conducted when Jack wasn't looking, which usually meant waiting for a day when he was away inspecting his sheep or on some similar mission.

In any case, by the time I'd been at Horsham a little more than a year I'd decided that if I was going to be mucking out stables and working a horse, I might as well be doing one of my own.

I well recall that at the time I was earning three pounds seven and six a week (the equivalent today of $6.75) and I reckoned I could afford maybe 20 or 25 pounds to get a horse.

Even then you couldn't get much for that sort of money, so I arranged with a friend (who knew considerably more about horses than I did) to 'go halves'.

We decided to go to the Wright Stephensons' winter mixed sale but unfortunately a few days beforehand he was injured in a horse-related accident and finished up in hospital.

So I went to the sale by myself.

As anyone who knew 'Minyip Jack' McKay would know, it would be impossible to be around him for long without absorbing at least a basic knowledge of Standardbred breeding, so I was all right on that score and recognised from a look in the catalogue that the unbroken two-year-old filly by Noble Scott from the Silver Peak mare Romantic Silver, a granddaughter of Walla Walla, was pretty well bred.

So I went and had a look at her.

She certainly was no 'oil painting' but she had four legs, one on each corner, and there didn't seem to be anything wrong with them, or with anything else so far as my untrained eye could spot immediately.

In retrospect I realise that had I not been quite so impatient I might have got her for less than 40 guineas ($84) as my bid turned out to be the only one.

Nevertheless, suddenly I was the owner of a horse (or part-owner anyway), so I hitch-hiked back to Horsham quite proud of myself and a couple of days later went and collected her from her own personal cattle truck at the railway station and walked her through the back streets of the town to her new home, in a stable at the Showgrounds.

It was a few days before my friend was discharged from hospital and by that time Helen had been wormed, cleaned and fed to the extent that her appearance had improved considerably.

He took one look at her and almost had a heart attack.

'You don't expect me to give you 20 guineas for that, do you?' he exclaimed.

Suddenly I was the sole owner of a horse, but I was also short of 20 guineas I had been depending on to buy some gear.

To make a long story short (or shorter, anyway), veteran Horsham horseman Les Jones came to my rescue, loaning me a set of harness and hopples and a few months later Helen was ready to race.

Her first start was at her home track and I will remember it as long as I live.

It was not only her first race but also my first race drive and I didn't have the slightest idea how either of us was likely to react once we got out there under the lights.

But even getting there seemed for a while that it might be a problem.

Helen – whose racing name for the first few starts of her career was Helen Of Troy – put on an act in the mounting yard, breaking a hopple carrier, which was hastily repaired with a piece of hayband.

Not being too sure about anything, I invested not a solitary shilling on her, so it came as something of a surprise that, when I pulled her out from midfield in the back-straight the last time, she suddenly grabbed the bit and began to swoop on the leading group of four, who had got away in front.

In the circumstances it seemed unwise to go three-wide around the last turn, so we headed back for the rails and eventually went to the line in a pocket, finishing fifth to Sampson Direct, who later turned out to be a pretty handy horse.

At her next start, around the two and a half furlong 'saucer' at Ararat, Helen drew the second row in a field of 14, got flattened at the start and was never in the race, finishing second-last to Baroda's Return.

With the two races 'under her belt' Helen was starting to learn what it was all about and her work started to indicate that she had enough ability to win a race.

But I was determined that if she did, it was I who was going to get the benefit and not all the 'smarties' who hung around the Horsham Showgrounds, and who had virtually queued up with my former partner to ridicule the bag of bones I had brought home from the sale.

So I let them think I was giving her an easy time, only ever letting them see her doing light jog work.

In the meantime, however, I was getting up early on 'fast mornings', riding Max's wife's bike to the track and working Helen while it was still dark.

She got to the stage that I thought she was going pretty well, then one day I got Max to come and have a drive on her to see if I was on the right track or merely going mad.

We worked her 'outside the hurdles' (which were put up to protect the inside of the track) in the middle of the afternoon when there was no-one around.

I can't remember exactly what time she worked, but I do recall that it equalled the track record, which at that time was held by top-line free-for-all performer Rising Flood.

Max and I were beginning to get hopeful, but we had to be sure.

So we took Minyip Jack into our confidence and the following week, watched only by the crows, we trialled three horses together at the Sheep Hills racecourse.

Jack drove Newport Dream, who at that time was a metropolitan class free-for-all horse, Max drove the rising star of Jack's stable, a filly named Skirl, and I drove Helen.

Newport Dream beat Helen by about a neck, with Skirl back in the dust. We had a winner – all we had to do was get a run somewhere and draw a decent barrier.

Our chance came on Boxing Day, 1963. Helen drew No 3 in a field of 15 with a ready-made favourite in Cita Sea, a smart filly who was later the dam of an even smarter one, Cita Dollar.

It was then that I did one of the few really smart things I've done in my life.

Despite the fact that I loved driving and would have 'killed' to have driven a winner, I swallowed my pride and decided that as Max knew more about driving than I did and I knew more about punting than he did, we'd better do it that way.

Jack agreed to the plan and scratched his two runners to leave Max free to drive Helen and me free to organise the betting.

I rounded up all the money I had in the world, which amounted at that time to 52 pounds, 'conned' a lift to Charlton for myself and my horse, and set off in quest of fame and fortune, or fortune anyway.

The short version of what happened is that we backed Helen from 33-1 to 6-4 and she did the rest, jumping straight to the front and leading throughout for an easy win.

It had cost me a pound to 'pay up', I had kept a pound to start my life again if anything went wrong, and had the rest on Helen.

I was earning about 170 pounds a year at the time. My winnings, 612 pounds, represented about three and a half years' pay.

Later in the afternoon a prominent owner came and offered me 800 pounds for my filly.

I was certainly younger and possibly sillier in those days, but I well remember my reply.

'Mate,' I said, 'I've got more money than I knew there was in the world – what would I do with another 800 pounds?'

At times we all have occasion to think of what one event has provided the highlight of our lives. There has never been much doubt about mine.

Helen went on to record four wins and 18 placings from about 40 starts before suffering horrific injuries in a training fall at the old Ballarat track one morning when she was a five-year-old.

There had been a football match there the day before and Max, who had moved to Ballarat and was training her at the time, had gone around beforehand with his workmate, clearing the leftover cans off the track.

Unfortunately they had missed one; Helen jumped it and came down 'like a ton of bricks'.

Her injuries, without going into them in gory detail, were such that the vet wanted to put her down.

But Max and his wife, Bev, insisted on at least trying to save her.

For several weeks Helen's life teetered ominously close to death's door but gradually it became apparent that all the work, the nursing and the care were going to pay off.

Eventually she came home to Yarrambat, where I was living at the time, and finally the last dressing came off exactly a year from the date of her fall.

Helen carried the grim reminders of her accident for the rest of her life but she nevertheless was able to go to stud, producing two winners, Skylarkin and Top Flat, both by Aachen.

Top Flat won numerous races, including three at Harold Park in Sydney and several in the US, while their sister, Aix La Chapelle, went to stud without racing and produced handy performer Aix La Charisse and Tipperary Sky, the dam of former top juvenile Tipawin.

Not much of that is relevant, though, because I promised Helen that day at Charlton that she had a home for life, and whether or not she had foals was never going to make any difference to that.

I am well aware that some of the more cynical of my colleagues – and perhaps our readers, too – will brand this story what one I can think of so graphically describes as 'self-indulgent wank', but I couldn't give a damn.

I know that for everyone who thinks that, there will be dozens who at some stage of their lives have had a 'special' horse, whom they loved, and who will be able to identify with this story.

Helen was not a champion, but we came a long way together and I have little doubt that but for her I would have drifted out of harness racing and would not be where I am today.

She was a lovely horse, who changed my life.

I have no doubt that of all the people who have ever had the experience of knowing and loving a horse, most have a tale they could tell.

This has been mine.

Copyright Acknowledgments

Without You, *But Once* and *In the Velvet Night* were first performed on Radio 3UZ, Melbourne.

When Did The Roses Die? and *Corporate Irrelevance* were first performed on Radio 3AW, Melbourne.

The Tree On Gibbet Hill was first published in The Australian Way, Qantas Airways.

Life's Path, But Once, The Tree On Gibbet Hill, When Did The Roses Die?, Without You, While Love Remains and *Corporate Irrelevance* were previously published in *More Lives Than One*.

Both *The Race* and *Catherine In Wonderland* won prizes in the 2005 edition of the Alan Marshall Short Story Awards.

www.ingramcontent.com/pod-product-compliance
Lightning Source LLC
Chambersburg PA
CBHW032106280426
43661CB00110B/1391/J